THE
SPINNING MIND

A Fun and Interactive Devotional
for Teens and Youth Leaders

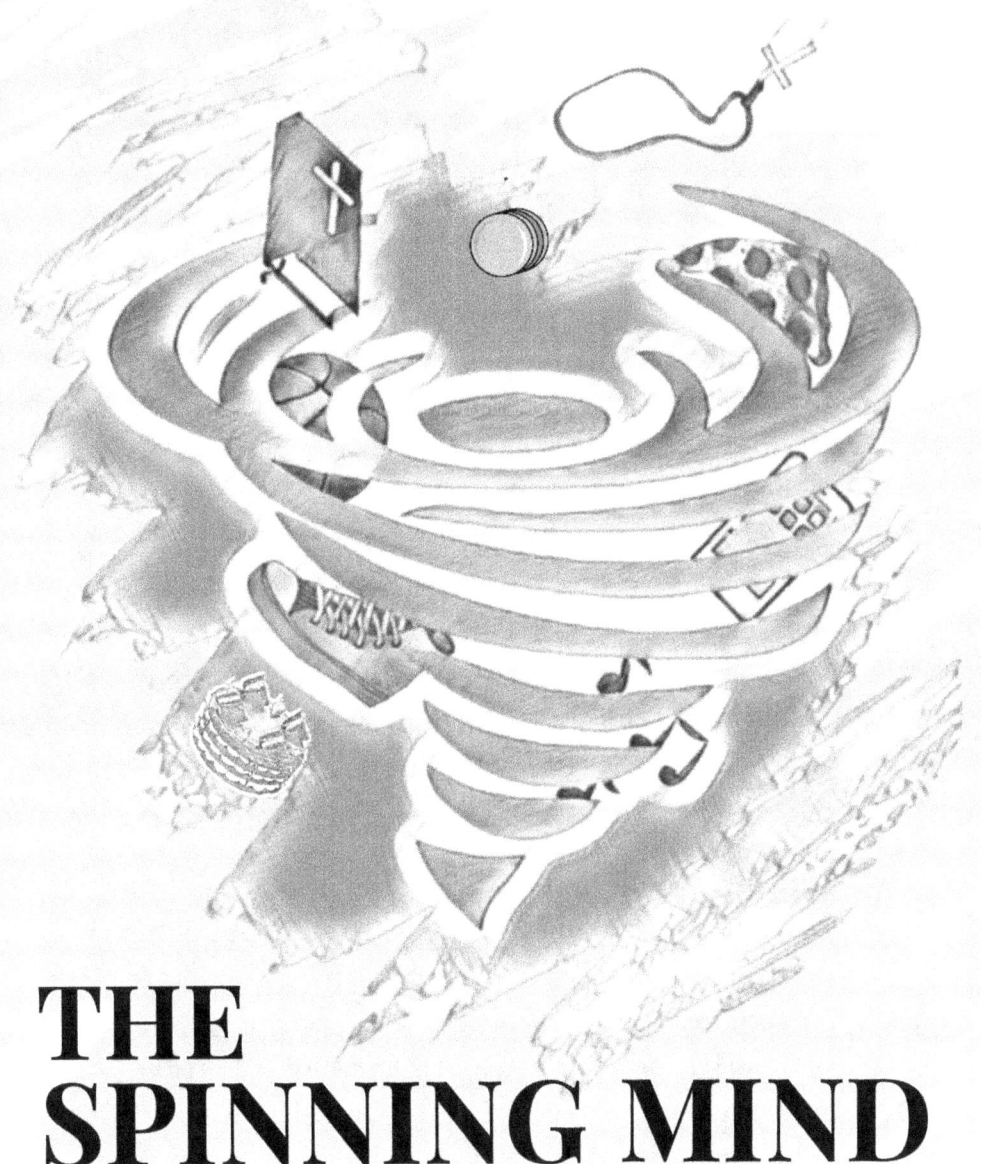

THE SPINNING MIND

A Fun and Interactive Devotional for Teens and Youth Leaders

SARAH JANE COOMBS

This book is dedicated to the young men and women who crossed my path in youth ministry and to those of you who still travel that journey with me today. Many of you have unknowingly inspired and motivated me as it was my heartfelt desire to do that very thing for you.
~Pastor Sarah

"And I pray that you, being rooted and established in love, may have power, together with all the Lord's holy people, to grasp how wide and long and high and deep is the love of Christ, and to know this love that surpasses knowledge—that you may be filled to the measure of all the fullness of God."
Ephesians 3:17-19

Endorsements

As someone with over two decades of experience in Christian leadership and a deep commitment to mentoring young people, I find Sarah's insights both inspiring and profoundly practical. This book serves as a valuable resource for anyone dedicated to nurturing the spiritual and personal growth of the next generation. This book is set apart by the practical exercises it offers, providing readers not just knowledge, but actionable steps to effectively engage. Sarah Jane's authentic storytelling and unwavering faith shine through every page, making this a must-read for students and youth leaders everywhere.

Major Lee-Ann van Duinen ~MA in Leadership, Certified Leadership Coach, Educator, and Salvation Army Officer (clergy)

Having worked with students and within student ministry for years I really enjoyed *The Spinning Mind Devotional*. In it, Sarah Jane takes us through the highs and lows of walking in relationship with Jesus in a fresh, fun way. This devotional is relevant, honest, and challenging, in a good way. I loved the reflections and the practical application of some of scriptures' deepest truths. Sarah Jane's openness and transparency about stories from her life serve to encourage and challenge students as they learn to live their faith in a practical way.

Pastor Wayne Giroux~Director of Student Ministries,

Western Ontario District PAOC

An empowering and eye-opening book, highly recommended and much needed for today's teens and youth leaders. This is the book I needed as a teen trying to understand my identity in Christ. Read this book if you want answers to how to discover your purpose.

Yvonne Odai ~ Kids Ministry Director, Teacher in Secondary Education, Former High School Guidance Counselor

This Teen Devotional offers a deeply encouraging journey for young readers seeking a closer connection with God. Through thought-provoking questions, engaging activities, and insightful guidance, Coombs skillfully navigates the complexities of discerning God's calling. This resource proves invaluable for both youths and young adults grappling with these profound questions, providing a reliable roadmap to understand and embrace God's direction in their lives."

Pastor Sarah Burt~Family Ministries Director, Clearview community church

Contents

Chapter 1

Jumpin' off the Page

Bright stage lights flashed through the wooden beams while giant speakers surrounded by hay bales blasted upbeat worship music. A hundred-twenty students and leaders from across Northern Ontario danced to the beat of the live band playing in the loft of our barn, stirring up dust as they jumped up and down on the dirt floor. I stepped outside the sliding barn door and called in a few more teenagers that were bouncing balls on the old cement pad that we called a basketball court. I had a heart for these teens; a deep passion was growing within me.

When did this all start? I don't really know; maybe in the high school library. I'm not sure which teacher sent us there—probably my English teacher. She was young and had short, bright red hair, which was ironic since her name was Ms. White. I always found Ms. White to be a little more creative and a little less traditional than the other high school teachers. That's what makes me think that she's the teacher who sent us to the library on this soul-searching assignment. The assignment was to answer a specific question—a question with the potential to excite or exhaust any teenager, any day, anywhere. The question was, "What do you want to do with your life?"

The assignment was to flip through magazines and newspapers looking for job descriptions or career opportunities that we would possibly want to do when we grew up—maybe an ad that got us excited about what might come next when our high school years were over. I remember flipping open a huge newspaper page that took up half the round library table. The page was filled with help wanted and career choices. It definitely wasn't a local paper. I grew up in Northern Ontario, and there was no way all those jobs were available in my hometown. It looked like a big city newspaper to me. I glanced up and down the columns looking for something that interested me. *Nope, nope, nope, uh, uh, nope,* nothing. I changed newspapers and looked through magazines, but I wasn't interested in any of those career choices. I may have ripped out a couple of "just in case I don't find anything good" kind of ads to use in my assignment, but nothing jumped off the page at me. Nothing really grabbed my attention and said, "Hey, this is what you want to do with your life." Then I saw it.

The ad said, "Youth counselor services." At the time, I had no idea what that really was, but the word "youth" did jump off the page at me as if it was printed in bold, italics, underlined, and perhaps even flashing in neon. The word "youth" stirred up something inside of me and still does to this day.

As I said, I had no idea what youth counseling service was, but I knew what I wanted it to be.

When I was a kid, my favorite place, other than home, was Newport, a summer camp in the Muskoka area. It was a three-hour trip to get there, but I was there every chance I got, from summer camps to youth events, winter retreats to leadership training. If there was camp, I was there. At fourteen, I took my counselor-in-training course. We called it C.I.T for short. Being a C.I.T was a moment of transition— too cool to still be a camper but not cool enough to be called staff. I passed my C.I.T. course, signed on as staff, and took up residence at the camp every summer until I got married; literally, I had my wedding there.

Every summer, I had the same job: a girls' counselor. I counseled both junior and senior girls, but senior girls were my favorite. It was less like babysitting and more like having a significant impact on their lives.

I knew that youth counselor services couldn't possibly mean being a camp counselor as a full-time career, but this was the job post that jumped off the page, so this is the job post I ripped out and glued into my assignment. Did Ms. White enjoy my presentation? Did she give me a good grade? I have no idea. I'm less impressed with the impact the assignment had on my grades than the significant impact it had on my life. It was a defining moment. A jump-off-the-page realization. I wanted to work with youth. Youth, teenagers, high school students, whatever you call them—these are the young people that I realized had and still have a special place in my heart.

On paper, the "what you want to do with your life" assignment was done and handed in, but in reality, it was just beginning. New task, answer this: what was the grown-up version of a camp counselor?

One of the lessons I teach over and over again to the young people I work with is that they were created with a purpose and that God has given them different gifts and talents that make them uniquely designed for a reason. If you have a passion for something, a non-stop desire to accomplish a certain task, a jump-off-the-page word in your life, then consider that God may be leading you into the very thing that you were designed for. There in the high school library, at the age of 15 or 16, I realized that working with teenagers was the direction in which God was leading me. A passion for student ministry started growing within me.

Maybe you have never had a "jump-off-the-page" experience in your life, and perhaps you never will, but without a doubt, God *is* calling you. He has a purpose and a plan for your life just like he did mine, just like he does for everyone.

"For we are God's handiwork, created in Christ Jesus to do good works, which God prepared in advance for us to do" (Ephesians 2:10 NIV).

Read chapter 1 of "The Spinning Mind of a Volunteer Youth Leader" for Sarah Jane's full 'Jumpin' off the Page' story.

Circle on the scale of 1-10 how afraid or excited you feel about God having a plan for your life, with 1 being afraid and 10 being excited.

Knowing that God has a purpose and a plan can be extremely comforting or it could be confusing. Maybe you're wondering, "What if I never figure it out?" "How will I know what God wants me to do?" "What if I don't hear him when he calls me?" or here's a big one, "What if God calls me to something I hate?"

If you have ever asked yourself any of these questions, or if you are asking them now, you're not alone.

> 10 out of 10 Christian teens, when asked, had questions about God's plan for their lives.

If you had one question about God's plan for your life, what would it be?

Let's tackle some of these questions together.

What if I never figure out God's plan for me?

You're figuring it out right now! Did God hide the plans for your life in a secret vault and forget to give you the key? No, He did not. It's not a secret, and the key to unlocking God's plan for your life is this:

Don't stress; just start working on the plans He has already given you.

How do I know what God wants me to do with my life?

It might not be jumping off the page, but it is definitely written down on one.

The Bible is full of God's plans for your life, from restoring your relationship with Him to being a light in your community so that others can find Jesus. It's all there!

Look up the following Bible verses and write down some of the plans that God has for your life.

His plan for you starts here. Your relationship with Him:

John 3:16 _____

1 John 1:9 _____

What's next?

Matthew 22:37 _____

Matthew 5:16 _____

1 Peter 5:6-7 _____

1 Peter 2:9 _____

1 Corinthians 10:31 _____

1 Thessalonians 5:16-18 _____

If you are looking for a more specific plan from God, you may find yourself asking, **"What if I don't hear God when he tells me what to do?"**

Don't worry about that; He's God. He has ways of getting people's attention. If you're waiting for God's instructions to show up with booming thunder or a crash of lightning, well, it could happen, but chances are it won't.

Sometimes the voice of God is loud, jumpin' off the page or spinning in your mind, but more often, God speaks to us in a quiet, gentle voice.

Need help hearing God's voice? You got it! Read John 14:26

Who will help you hear God's voice?

The closer you are to God the more you learn to recognize His voice. The Bible says we are like sheep (John 10:27). The voice of a stranger might freak out the sheep, but they recognize the shepherd's voice. So, instead of running away, they follow him. When you spend time talking to God and practicing listening, you will learn to recognize the voice of the Holy Spirit leading you.

If you want specific directions from God, then keep asking, keep listening, and keep following him until you can recognize His voice. Until then, keep working on the plans that God has already written down for you.

What if I hate God's plan for me?

You won't! Will God call you to something scary? Maybe! Out of your comfort zone? All the time. Beyond your own abilities? Yep! But the Bible says in Ephesians 2:10:

> *For we are God's handiwork, created in Christ*
> *Jesus to do good works, which God prepared*
> *in advance for us to do.*

You know what else God prepared in advance? You! We were all created with different gifts, talents, and abilities. We are all uniquely designed for a reason. God will use those gifts, talents and abilities to accomplish His plan.

Make a list of your talents, abilities, and things you love to do even if you're not that good at them.

Sometimes other people can see things in us that we can't see in ourselves. Send a message to three friends right now and ask them to name two things that you are good at or have fun doing. Add their responses to your list.

"If you have a passion for something, a non-stop desire to accomplish a certain task, a jump off the page word in your life, then consider that God may be leading you into the very thing that you were designed for."
~Sarah Jane

Choose three skills, talents, or passions from your list and brainstorm why God might have given you those specific abilities or desires.
How could you be using those abilities or desires to honor God right now?

Prayer Break

Thank God for any passions or interests He has laid on your heart. Pray that He will give you opportunities to use your skills and abilities to honour Him.
Ask God to help you hear and listen to His voice.
Remember that God has already written down important plans for you throughout the Bible. Pray that God will continue to show you His plans as you read through His word.

Chapter One Notes

Chapter 2

Detours and Side Roads

Everyone was taking their turn, and now it was mine. In alphabetical order, all the grade 12 students were called to the guidance office. When I walked in, the table was covered with course catalogs for all the colleges in Ontario. The guidance counselor was ready with her clipboard. She was going to talk me through and help me decide the "furthering your education" process. That wasn't necessary; I already knew exactly what I wanted to do.

Considering the word *youth* had jumped off the page at me, I now had a plan. I was going to Bible college. I was going to graduate with my social work degree, and I was going to work with teens. That was the plan. I guess the guidance counselor was happy with that because she didn't try to talk me out of it.

I didn't need to go back to the guidance office for a follow-up meeting. I had everything figured out, or so I thought.

Two summers before high school graduation, I met Zip. His real name is Tim, but he was the instructor on the zipline at camp, so everyone called him Zip. Zip and I were married at the camp the summer I graduated high school.

Zip had been offered a job at the London, Ontario airport, and we were headed off to the city. If you had asked me a year before, I would not have thought that I would be living in London. The Bible college was in Winnipeg, Manitoba. There were 2000 km between where I was and where I thought I would be. I had a plan, and I thought it was a good one. A year and a half earlier, before I met with the counselor in the school guidance office, I had marked out a path of where I felt God was leading me and how I thought I would get there. The path I was on seemed to be taking me in an entirely different direction. I still wanted to do youth ministry, but I wasn't sure how that was going to happen.

Our first apartment was only blocks away from Fanshawe College. There were two months until fall classes started. It was the last minute, but I thought maybe if I applied right away, I might get accepted for school in the fall. I applied for their child and youth worker program. I was hoping to get started working with youth, but all I got was a rejection letter. I knew that God had called me to youth ministry of some kind, but I had no idea how I was going to get there. I no longer had a plan or a path marked out to take me where I thought that I should be, but I was trusting God. I knew that the Bible said to "trust in the Lord with all your heart and lean not on your own understanding, in all your ways submit to Him and he will make your paths straight" (Proverbs 3:5-6 NIV).

Over the next few years, my path to youth ministry was full of detours and side roads. The church in London asked me to take over the children's program. It wasn't youth, but it was a start. It was easy, and I had extra time on my hands. I told Zip I either needed to get a job or start a family. I think God heard us, chuckled, and said, "How about both?" I liked helping at the church and didn't want to stop, but when Zip's dad died, baby Victoria and I moved with Zip to his hometown where he took over his dad's trucking business and was away more than he was home.

I wasn't happy; I missed being together as a family. I was lying in my bed one night, thinking about how unhappy I was. I began to pray. I was giving God a piece of my mind. I know; I should have been praying for patience or wisdom or something like that. The right thing to do probably would have been to pray for direction and guidance, but I didn't. He gave it to me anyway.

I felt an overwhelming sense of urgency inside of me. I leaned off the side of my bed as far as I could without losing my balance and falling on my head. I was reaching for a box of things that were still packed from our move several months before. I slid my hand into the box and pulled out an old Bible college catalog that I had been holding onto since high school.

My heart was racing as I held the course catalog in

my hand. I knew it was time. This was really going to happen. I applied for the social work program. I was sending a last-minute college application again, but this time I got accepted. We loaded my car on the back of Zip's transport trailer and headed west. I felt as if God had taken me on several detours but that I was now on the straight path to youth ministry. I was wrong.

After the first semester, I started experiencing morning sickness. The doctor at the drop-in clinic gave me a stern lecture about teen pregnancy and being a single mom. I didn't bother telling him that I wasn't a teenager, I wasn't single, and this wasn't my first pregnancy. It was just too much fun watching him make a fool of himself. Regardless of his terrible bedside manner, he was able to confirm that there was a baby growing inside of me. I finished off my first year but wasn't going back in September.

Zip had been offered a job as a flight instructor at the Lindsay airport. He had decided to sell the truck and work close to home where he could spend more time with Victoria and baby Benjamin. Zip's aviation plans were back on track; my youth ministry ones, not so much.

It wasn't long before I was offered a volunteer position at the church in Lindsay. Guess what they asked me to do? Yep, I had been asked to run the children's program. Did I have an "I want to work with kids" tattoo on my forehead, or what? I accepted the position; it wasn't youth ministry but I was happy to help out where I was needed. When the teen class teacher moved away, I started working with junior and senior high students. I really felt like God was using me to make a difference, but I soon discovered that the twists and turns in my path to youth ministry weren't over yet. Zip had applied for a job as a pilot in Kapuskasing, Ontario, and we would be moving once again.

Youth ministry didn't look very promising in our new church. There was no youth programming, and there were only four kids the first Sunday we attended. It wasn't long before we learned our pastors were leaving. They asked if I would be willing to take over the children's ministry. I really did believe that God was leading me into youth ministry, but every path we took seemed to lead us to the doorstep of a church that needed someone to run their children's program. I said yes, and that was the start of an amazing 22 years of ministry in Kapuskasing.

What began with a children's program grew into an entire ministry for children, families, junior high kids, and youth. Yes, youth! I was exactly where I wanted to be, and it was worth every twist and turn along the way. When I think about the Bible verse that says when you trust in the Lord that he will make your paths straight, I have to shake my head, smirk, and say, "Ok, God, that path was anything but straight." I realize the verse is really talking about guiding and directing your path, and *that* he certainly did.

> **Trust in the Lord with all your heart and lean not on your own understanding; in all your ways submit to him, and he will make your paths straight (Proverbs 3:5-6 NIV).**

Read Chapter 2, "Getting There" of "The Spinning Mind of a Volunteer Youth Leader" for Sarah Jane's full story of detours and side roads.

Check off which of the following best describes you!

☐ I'm good with living in chaos.
☐ A little scattered-brained sometimes.
☐ Organized sometimes, other times not so much.
☐ I like to keep things organized
☐ I'm a "make a plan, stick to the plan" kind of person

What questions have you been asked about your future?

_____

_____

_____

_____

Living out God's plan for your life might be full of side roads and detours. What three things does Proverbs 3:5-6 say you should do if you want God to direct your path?

_____, _____, _____

Why should we not lean on our own understanding? (Isaiah 55:8-9)

"Hey, wait, if following Jesus is full of twists and turns and detours, then how do we know what's next?

Maybe you won't; following Jesus is stepping out in faith, believing that even when you don't know what's next, God does. Living out God's plan for your life means every day loving Him, serving Him, and trusting Him. Even when you don't know what's next.

It was potluck Sunday. I brought a loaf of peanut butter and jam sandwiches and a cake. The cake was decorated nicely and wrapped in saran wrap. I set the cake up on the dash of the van and was holding the peanut butter sandwiches on my lap. As we were driving along our back road, my husband said, "Hold the cake." I said, "I don't need to hold the cake; it's o.k. on the dash." Without any explanation, he repeated himself, "Hold the cake." Now, I'm the kind of person that doesn't really like to be told what to do. If someone asks me nicely to do something, OK no problem, but if someone has a habit of telling me what to do, then I sometimes have a habit of…saying no. Yes, I know, I really should work on that. But when my husband said, "Hold the cake," I said, "No." He said it again: "Hold the cake." With as much attitude as I could muster, I took the cake, put it in the palm of my hand, and held it up in the air. "Ok, I'm holding the cake." He goes on to say, "Use two hands." So I took my pointer finger and placed it on the very edge of the plate. "Fine, two hands," I exclaimed.

Now, there is a spot on the road that moves as the frost comes in and out of the ground. Sometimes it's flat but sometimes there's a giant bump in the road. Tim had been down the road already and he knew that the seasonal bump was back. That's why he said, "Hold the cake!" We hit that bump, and the peanut butter and jam sandwiches went flying up in the air, along with the cake. The sandwiches landed on the floor, but my husband reached over and put his hand on the side of the cake. He had to save the cake because there was no way I was going to rescue the cake with the one finger that I was using to hold it. I didn't know we were going to hit a bump. He didn't tell me that we were going to hit a bump. He just said, "Hold the cake." If I had known what was coming, or seen what was ahead, then I would have listened. I would have done what I was supposed to do if I had only known what was coming next.

Hold the cake moment

Hold the cake moment definition:

When you need to step out in faith and follow Jesus, not knowing what's next.

When God asks you to do something and you don't know why.

Make this mug cake, and then write about the "hold the cake moments" you have had in your life.

Mug Cake

4 tablespoons flour

2 tablespoons granulated sugar

½ teaspoon baking powder

4 tablespoons milk

1 ½ tablespoons vegetable oil

¼ teaspoon vanilla

a handful of sprinkles

or chocolate chips

Mix it in a big mug and cook for 45 seconds-1 minute in the microwave. Careful, it's hot! Enjoy!

_____

_____

_____

_____

The Bible is full of "hold the cake" moments where people need to step out in faith and follow Jesus, not knowing what's next. The apostle Paul in the book of Acts had a "hold the cake" moment. Paul had a plan. He planned to travel around the east side of the Mediterranean Sea, preaching and teaching in the large towns and cities along the way.

What was Paul's "hold the cake" moment? (Acts 16:6-8)

_____

_____

Paul had a plan, but the Spirit of God had a better plan. Paul couldn't see beyond that moment, but God could. Paul needed to trust God even if he didn't understand, even if he didn't know what was next.

FYI

After Paul was led away from Bithynia and the province of Asia Minor
~he has a vision of a man from Macedonia calling him there (Acts 16:9).
~he met up with Luke, who recorded this part of history for us (Acts 16:10).
~the apostle Peter taught the people in Bithynia and Asia(1 Peter 1:1).
God knows what He's doing!

There are going to be times in your life where God does things that you don't understand and you need to follow Jesus even when you have no idea where he is leading you. When you have your own "hold the cake" moments, trust God to lead you in the right direction.

"When you're trusting God, but the path that you are on doesn't lead you straight to where you think he is calling you to, don't worry. He's just taking you for an adventure along the way."
~Sarah Jane

Write in your own words what Proverbs 3:5-6 **says:**

Prayer Break

Pray and ask God to direct your path. Ask Him to help you to make good decisions. Tell God that you want to trust Him more even when you don't know what's next, and ask Him to help you do that.

Chapter Two Notes

Chapter 3

Open Heart Policy

When Zip and I were first married, we started a college and careers group. We lived in a small two-bedroom apartment on the seventh floor. Every Monday night, we would open the doors to young adults. Zip would prepare a lesson. I would make sure the apartment was clean, the cookies were baked, and a jug of lemonade was ready. Since then, we have had many different homes, yet the doors have remained open.

After our move to Kapuskasing, while Zip flew the skies over Northern Ontario, I began to volunteer, first with children and then with youth. It wasn't until I started volunteering with teens again that God helped us to transform our open-door policy into an open-heart policy, and the teens I worked with became a part of our family.

I was recently asked to guest-speak at our home church. They were in the middle of a series about teamwork, and I was asked to preach from the book of Acts, a message on the early church and what made them such a great team. As I prepared the message, I was reminded how followers of Jesus had learned about God together, prayed together, hung out with each other all the time, took care of each other, and ate meals together in their homes. Basically, they lived life together as one big family. This is an excellent example for us today. Digging into the Bible together, praying together, hanging out, taking care of each other, not just within the walls of a church, but really living life together.

We had started living life together with our students. It was never a conscious decision; it just happened. We loved the students and didn't mind sharing our lives with them. Zip was a soccer guy; he played for the Kapuskasing Longhorns, and they had games after church during the summer. Zip would sneak off right after the last song and change into his soccer uniform in the front seat of his pickup truck in order to make it to his game on time. I would load up the minivan, pick up a couple of family meals at the grocery store, and head over to the soccer field for the afternoon. There was an open invitation for any teens who wanted to join us. They always did. I don't know if it was the thrill of the game or the smell of chicken tenders and potato wedges, but youth always showed up. Chances are it wasn't the game or the family meal deal that kept them coming, but the opportunity to hang out together as one big family.

One Sunday afternoon, we invited the youth to come to the farm and do hay with us. When people think of doing chores on the farm, unless they've lived the farm life, they tend to get confused between fantasy and reality. They picture radiant sunbeams streaming through the open loft doors while young people in jean overalls and cowboy boots move fluffy piles of wheat with a pitchfork from one end of the loft to the other. Children swing on ropes and land on piles of loose hay, and the farmer squirts milk at the kittens while milking the cows. *That's the fantasy*. We invited the youth to help bring in the hay. The bales are heavy, the hay scratches, the loft is uncomfortably hot on sunny days, the hay elevator is extremely noisy, and the air is thick with hay dust. That is the reality. We told them it would be hard work and that the only payment would be unlimited glasses of lemonade.

I expected a couple of students to rise to the challenge, but what I didn't expect was that there would be 17 people working in the hay that day, including one teenage girl with a broken leg. We even had some parents join in. The parents reminisced about working on a farm as kids and talked about how it's good for the teens to experience some old-fashioned hard work. The students who showed up that day weren't there for the hard work. They didn't come for the lemonade or to jump from a swinging rope onto a pile of hay (we actually *did* have that part of the fantasy). They were there because they were part of a family, a team. We had become a group of people who relied on each other and helped each other out. We were living life together. What had started as an open-door policy has changed over the years. It wasn't just ministries and programs that were a part of our family life but the students themselves. They became a part of our everyday lives. Just like the church in the book of Acts, we were a team living life together.

"And all the believers met together constantly and shared everything with each other" (Acts 2:44).

Read Chapter 3 in "The Spinning Mind of a Volunteer Youth Leader" for Sarah Jane's full experience of living with an open-heart policy.

What teams, clubs or groups are you in?

If you could join any kind of team, what would it be?

If you could create your own team, what would it look like?

We find a great example of what a team of people following Jesus should look like in Acts chapter 2. Acts is the fifth book in the New Testament. The first four books, Matthew, Mark, Luke, and John, all talk about the life of Jesus, who He was, His birth, His teachings, the miracles He did, His death on the cross, His forgiveness—everything you need to know about Jesus. The Book of Acts is all about what happened next. It explains how followers of Jesus exploded from 125 people to over 3,000 people in one day and gives us a pretty cool example of what teamwork with other people who believe in Jesus should look like.

Read Acts 2:42-47 and make a list of all the things that the followers of Jesus did together.

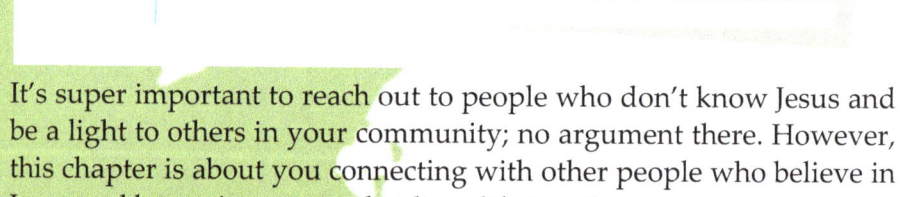

It's super important to reach out to people who don't know Jesus and be a light to others in your community; no argument there. However, this chapter is about you connecting with other people who believe in Jesus and becoming a team that lives life together.

Example of Teamwork from Acts

1. What they did: devoted to the apostles' teachings

The apostles weren't the recognized religious authorities of the time. They were fishermen, tax collectors, ordinary guys, but the church wanted to know what these guys were saying because they were talking about Jesus. They lived life with Jesus, He was their teacher. Jesus trained them, and the apostles shared everything they learned with the new church, with the team.

We don't have Jesus' apostles here with us today, but we still have their teachings. They wrote them down for us—who Jesus was, what He did, what He said, His Life, His death, God's forgiveness through Him; it's all in there. The early church devoted themselves to the apostles' teachings, and as a member of "the team," the apostles' teachings are just as important to us today.

What can you do to devote yourself to the apostles' teachings?

2. What they Did: Fellowship

I used to think that fellowship meant hanging out together. I grew up going to church, and the fellowship hall was where all the cool stuff happened. That's where all the snacks were and where the youth group played games. If there was lunch after church, it would be in the fellowship hall. So, yeah, I thought fellowship meant hanging out and eating snacks. I was wrong. Fellowship is so much more than that. The church of Acts did hang together and eat snacks, but when they devoted themselves to fellowship, they were actually devoting themselves to each other.

Fellowship isn't just hanging out. It's more of a spiritual togetherness. They weren't just connected to Jesus, but because of Jesus, they were connected to each other.

What did fellowship look like for the believers in The Book of Acts? It looked like living life together.

What can you do to live life together with other followers of Jesus?

3. What they did: Shared meals together

Sharing a meal in the Bible was also called *breaking of bread*. It can mean either a time of communion where they break bread and remember what Jesus has done for them, or it can mean simply eating a meal together. The Bible talks about different times that people ate together, even the times that Jesus shared a meal. This is where things happened; they hung out together, they shared stories, and had deep discussions. Every meal was a time of fellowship.

Deep friendships can be formed by sharing a meal together. Social barriers can be broken down by sharing a meal together. Bonding as a team happens when we share a meal together.

What can you do to share meals together with other followers of Jesus?

4. What they did: Prayed

Prayer was extremely important to the church in Acts. They prayed *with* each other, and they prayed *for* each other. When we're talking about the early church as an example of teamwork, we see that this team prayed, and when they prayed, powerful things happened.

The first thing the followers of Jesus did after Jesus ascended to Heaven was get together and pray. If we are a Bible-believing, Jesus-following team, then the same God who powerfully responded to the prayers of the church in Acts will answer our prayers today.

What can you do when it comes to praying with and for other followers of Jesus?

5. What they did: Took care of each other's needs

Thousands of people had traveled to Jerusalem for the Jewish festival. Three thousand of them became followers of Jesus that day and didn't go home. They stayed in Jerusalem. They joined the team. But they had nothing. They only planned to be there for the festival, so they didn't bring their possessions with them. The followers of Jesus living in Jerusalem at the time took care of the new believers. They sold property and possessions to give to any other followers of Jesus who were in need.

What can you do to help take care of other followers of Jesus?

CHALLENGE

COMPLETE ✓

Invite a friend to finish this Bible study with you.

Fellowship/live life together, hang out with another follower of Jesus this week.

Invite a Christian friend over for dinner. Bonus if you cook it yourself!

Pray with or pray for someone today.

Think of another follower of Jesus who is in need and see what you can do to help.

Prayer Break

Pray and ask God to help you be a team player. Ask Him to show you different ways that you can live life together with other followers of Jesus. Ask God to show you opportunities to help other people who believe in Him.

Chapter Three Notes

Chapter 4

Runway Ranch

It was cold, and the back road I was driving down was covered with snow. Probably wasn't the best day to head out for a drive, but while the older kids were at school and Zip was at work, I packed up Levi, our youngest boy, in our blue Pontiac Montana and headed out.

I will always remember that drive to the farm. I pulled over on the side of the road in front of a white and green, fairly modest looking home with a *for sale* sign in the window. I would have pulled into the driveway, but no one was living there at the time, and the driveway wasn't plowed. There were two houses on the property, the main house, white with green shutters, and a smaller kind of beat-up-looking house with worn-out, blue-painted siding. There was a huge barn in the backyard, one section made of original barn board and a large addition made from lumber and tin. The farm had a grass strip runway in the field beside the house. We had been told it was there but hadn't seen it since the fields were covered with snow.

We had already put in an offer to buy the farm—a little crazy, considering that I had never seen the inside of the houses or the barn. The offer we put in on the house wasn't likely to be accepted. We offered half of the asking price. Half! Who does that? Zip does. He's a bargain hunter and never pays full price for anything if he can help it.

I hadn't planned to drive to the farm that day, but I felt drawn to it. I sat in the van on the side of the road, and I prayed. I'm pretty sure these are the exact words I prayed: "Dear God, if you give us this house, I'll use it for you." Was I in the habit of trying to strike a deal with God? Did I think I had some kind of leverage with the all-knowing, all-powerful creator of the universe? No, but that's what I said to Him. "If you give us this house, I'll use it for you."

I meant what I said. I could already picture it. A yard full of teenagers, bonfires, campouts, field games, Bible studies; so much potential. God did give us the farm with no counteroffer. That summer, we named our property and painted the name *Runway Ranch* in big, bold green letters across the front of the barn. I truly believe that what I thought was making a deal with God was really just agreeing to something that God had already planned out for us long before we saw a *for sale* sign in the window. I once heard a woman say that the best way to get her husband to do something she wanted was to let him think that it was his idea in the first place. I may or may not have tried this on Zip from time to time. Perhaps God was using this technique on me. Providing us with the perfect location for youth ministry, a potential home away from home for some of our students, and then allowing me to think that I came up with this idea on my own.

Runway Ranch was more than just a home for Zip, myself, and our now four children; it was a part of youth ministry, and I wouldn't have had it any other way. It didn't take long before I concluded that it was definitely God's idea, His plan. The Bible says that God is able to do immensely more than we could ever ask or even imagine. I never would have imagined such a powerful youth ministry would take place at Runway Ranch.

There is a futon in our rec room. The rec room isn't large. It's big enough for our pool table but not big enough so that the ends of the pool cues don't hit the wall when you're trying to take a shot. In the corner of the room is the futon; it's an old, beat-up, falling-apart futon. We all agree that it's time for the futon to go, but it just hasn't happened yet. The metal bars underneath the futon are broken, so we put pieces of wood under the mattress to stop your butt from falling through. The fabric on the mattress is torn, so we flipped it over, and the rips are on the bottom. Definitely time for the futon to go.

I'm not holding on to it for sentimental reasons, just practical ones. I don't have anything else for visitors to sleep on, and it will be a lot of work to carry that thing up the stairs and out the door. If I kept it for sentimental reasons, that would be totally understandable. That futon has played a huge part in our youth ministry at Runway Ranch. A lot of teens have slept on that not-so-comfortable futon. Some were just hanging out, maybe part of a girls' or guys' night out, crashing at Runway Ranch as part of a youth event, but for others, it really was a home away from home. More than just a place to sleep, for some, it was a refuge in the middle of the night; for others, a quiet place to be alone; and for some, it was an escape from the harsh realities of their lives, if only for one night. For others, that beat-up futon was a place to curl up and let the tears stream down their face until the sun rose in the morning and brought with it a brighter day.

The open-door, open-heart policy that we had tried to maintain over the years didn't only extend to our home at Runway Ranch but to the barn and the fields as well. If you wandered the backyard or fields at Runway Ranch at any given time, summer or winter, you would surely find evidence of a youth project somewhere. A makeshift campground, a path from snowshoes, a bush camp, a skidoo trail, a paintball bush, or a plastic Easter egg still hiding in the field when the snow finally melted at the end of April.

The barn at Runway Ranch was the location for many Northern Ontario Youth Rallies. One rally hosted over 100 young people scattered throughout the barn in a giant indoor hay maze. After escaping the maze, they watched the Cities Under Fire tour band play a concert from the loft. The barn concert is featured several times in the Cities Under Fire - Stay official music video on YouTube.

The Bible says that God can go above and beyond what we think is possible and that is exactly what He did.

God took our simple family farm and used it to do immensely more than we could have asked or imagined.

In chapter 1, you were asked to make a list of the skills, talents, or passions that God has given you. If you allow Him to, God can use those gifts and abilities to honor Him and make a difference in both your life and the lives of the people around you. What if God could use more than just your skills and abilities? What if He could use your possessions, the things you own, your stuff? Guess what? He can! Just like God used our family farm to make a powerful difference in people's lives; if you allow him to, He can use whatever you have and do the same thing.

"Now to him who is able to do immeasurably more than all we ask or imagine, according to his power that is at work within us" (Ephesians 3:20 NIV).

For more of the inspirational adventures of Runway Ranch, read chapter 4 in "The Spinning Mind of a Volunteer Youth Leader."

On a scale of 1-10, circle how active your imagination is. 1 being not active at all. "I've never been much of a dreamer," 10 being very active. "My imagination is stuck in overdrive."

1 2 3 4 5 6 7 8 9 10

Imagine and write down how each of the following objects could be used to honor God and make a difference in someone else's life.

_____   _____
_____   _____
_____   _____
_____
_____   _____
_____   _____
_____
_____   _____
_____   _____
_____   _____
_____   _____

Here are three stories from the Bible showing how God can take the ordinary things that we have and do even more than we could possibly ask or imagine. I have 'Sarahphrased' these stories for you, but the original version can be found in John 6, 1 Samuel 17 and 1 Kings 17.

What's In Your Lunch?

When Jesus was preaching, large clouds of people would follow Him. One time, they followed Him all day, skipping lunch and supper so they could stay and hang out with Him. Jesus wanted to feed the people, so He sent his disciples to see what they could find. The disciples found a young boy and said, "What's in your lunch?"

Read John 6:9. What did the boy have in his lunch?

Read John 6:10-12. What was Jesus able to do with what the boy had to offer?

What's In Your Backpack?

In 1 Samuel, there was a teen named David. His people were under attack from the Philistine army. David was a shepherd boy, not a soldier. He volunteered to fight against Goliath, the strongest soldier in the Philistine army. David asked himself, "What's in my backpack?"

Read 1 Samuel 17:40. What did David have in his backpack?

Read 1 Samuel 17:45-49.

With God's help, what was David able to accomplish with just a slingshot and a stone?

What's in your cupboard?

There was a man named Elijah who honored God and became a messenger to God's people. One day, he was walking across a land where the river had dried up and no food was growing in the fields. He met a woman and asked her for water and some bread. She said she had no bread to give him, so Elijah asked, "What's in your cupboard?"

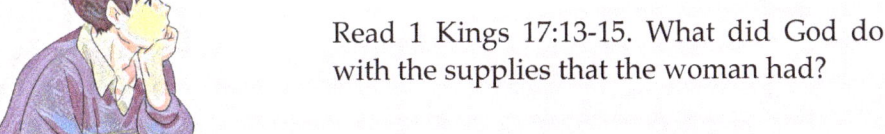

Read 1 Kings 17:7-12. What did the woman have in her cupboard?

Read 1 Kings 17:13-15. What did God do with the supplies that the woman had?

What's in your room?

Look around your room and make a list of what you own. Add other objects that your parents allow you to use.

Choose three things from your list and describe how you could use those items to honor God and make a difference in someone's life.

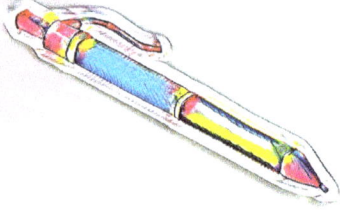

Don't let yourself be limited by what you think you can do on your own. Read Ephesians 3:20 (NIV) and fill in the blanks.

"Now to him who is able to do immeasurably more than_____

_____

_____

according to _____

_____".

Prayer Break

Talk to God. Thank Him for everything that you have. Ask God to help you to be creative and discover how you can use what you have to honor Him. Remember that God can do more than you could ever ask or imagine. Ask God to show you opportunities to honor Him and make a difference in the lives of others.

Chapter Four Notes

Chapter 5

More Where That Came From

As a mom, I often have moments where all I want is for my kids to do what I tell them to, when I tell them to. None of this, "after the game," "when this video is over," "I'm just going to grab a snack first." They might as well just say what they really mean. "I'll do it, but you're gonna have to ask me ten times first." I wonder if God ever feels this way about me.

I was sleeping in my old bedroom at my parents' house. Zip and I were there for a visit. In the middle of the night, I woke up with my brother's name in my head. I'd woken up with people's names in my head before, but this time it was different, more intense, a sit-up straight and gasp for air kind of wake-up call. I had been told that if God puts someone's name in your head you should pray for them. So, I did. I didn't know what to pray for, but I prayed. I prayed, "Dear God, please help my brother." What else could I pray? I didn't know what he needed prayer for, so "God, please help my brother" was what I prayed.

In the morning, we learned that my brother had lost control of the truck, driven off the road, and hit a rock face. He had been knocked out, and the truck was on fire. My brother woke up just in time to escape through the smashed back window and run to the road before the truck exploded. He described it like a scene from a movie; the entire truck lifted off the ground as it exploded into flames.

My brother's near-death experience was happening at the same time God had placed the very intense, pray-for-your-brother wake-up call. When the Spirit of God asks you to do something, He does it for a reason.

One evening, I needed a babysitter, so I asked a lady named Jackie. Jackie wasn't working at the time, so she didn't mind stopping by occasionally if I had a meeting. That evening, Jackie babysat for less than an hour. When it came time to pay her, I went to my room and pulled out a cash box I kept in the closet. I was running a photography business at the time, so I had plenty of cash on hand. I put the cash box on the bed and opened the lid to take out a $10 bill. There beside the ten-dollar bill was a one-hundred-dollar bill. I was getting pretty good at recognizing God's voice, and at that moment, he spoke to me. He said, "Give her the hundred-dollar bill." I know it was God and not me, because that definitely wasn't my idea. I didn't mind being generous, but a hundred dollars an hour for babysitting seemed a little excessive. I held up the ten dollars in one hand and the one hundred dollars in the other hand. God had clearly told me what to do, but was I willing to listen? I put the ten-dollar bill back in the cash box and gave Jackie the one-hundred-dollar bill. I said,

"God told me to give you this." Her response is the exact reason that we should always listen when God speaks. She started to cry, and as she hugged me, she said, "Thank you so much; I really needed this. Now I can pay my hydro bill." I had no idea that Jackie was struggling financially. But God did. He always knows.

I was starting to recognize more and more the voice of God in my life, but just like my kids, when I would give them a job to do, I didn't always listen right away. It's not that I'm a fan of procrastination. I'm usually a 'just get it done' kind of person, especially in youth ministry. When it came to hearing God's voice and taking action, I probably needed a lesson on timing.

Part of running youth ministry was speaking to the older teens every Friday night with important life lessons, inspirational messages, and creative devotions, all based on biblical truths. For a little while, I struggled to find something that I really felt passionate about and wanted to teach a series on. That's not actually true; I did have one really awesome idea that I couldn't wait to preach on. It was one of those God-inspired ideas that comes with all the extras. The message was called *The Big Picture*, and God had flooded my mind with Bible verses, inspirational stories, and object lessons. God had blessed me with this idea, and it was good. I was passionate about it. So passionate that I decided to save it.

I know that doesn't make sense, but I hosted larger

youth events throughout the year, and I really wanted to share something great at the next sectional youth
event. The big-picture message was great, so I saved it
and filed it in the back of my mind for another time. I
thought that was a good plan, but I was wrong. Week
to week, I was struggling to find something I really
thought would help the students, motivate them, and
encourage them. It was as if I had writer's block, but I
wasn't writing. I guess it was preacher's block. Is that
a thing?

Meanwhile, I had that very specific big-picture message that God had laid on my heart tucked away for
another time. At the next sectional youth event that I
hosted, I preached *The Big Picture*. It was good; it really
seemed to pack a punch for the students, just like I had
anticipated.

In the weeks following, I had no problem planning
lessons, messages, and devotions.

My mind was flooded with good ideas. I learned my
lesson. I never should have filed away *The Big Picture*.
I should have preached it. I should have used the idea
that God had given me when he gave it to me and not
six months later.

My mistake reminds me of the story of burying coins
found in the Bible in Matthew 25:14-30. The story of the
gold coins teaches that if you use what God gives you,
He will trust you with even more. I now have a mental
sticky note that goes along with any creative idea God

gives me. The note reads, "There's plenty more where that came from."

One of my boys came into my room the other day and told me he had an idea for me to preach to the youth. I told him that it was his idea, and he should preach it. He said, and I quote, "I'm not the youth pastor." I said maybe you could be. He said, "Nah, this is the only message I have." I confidently told him that if God had given him that message, he should use it and see what happens next. He shouldn't bury it away like the coins in the story; he should share it. If he does, he may discover plenty more where that came from.

Whether it's a creative message, an overpaid babysitter, or a midnight wake-up call with someone's name in your head, when God asks you to do something, He does it for a reason.

"His master replied, 'Well done, good and faithful servant! You have been faithful with a few things; I will put you in charge of many things. Come and share your master's happiness!'" (Matthew 25:21).

For more encouraging examples of hearing God's voice, read chapter 5, "More Where That Come From" in "The Spinning Mind of a Volunteer Youth Leader."

Circle how long it takes you to jump into action when you are asked to do the following:

Clean your room

Right away! As soon as I possibly can; Depends if I remember; Probably an hour; Maybe a week; After I get asked 10 times

Do your homework

Right away! As soon as I possibly can; Depends if I remember; Probably an hour; Maybe a week; After I get asked 10 times

Take out the trash

Right away! As soon as I possibly can; Depends if I remember; Probably an hour; Maybe a week; After I get asked 10 times

Text back

Right away! As soon as I possibly can; Depends if I remember; Probably an hour; Maybe a week; After I get asked 10 times

Pay back money

Right away! As soon as I possibly can; Depends if I remember; Probably an hour; Maybe a week; After I get asked 10 times

Say I'm sorry

Right away! As soon as I possibly can; Depends if I remember; Probably an hour; Maybe a week; After I get asked 10 times

Wash your sweaty gym clothes

Right away! As soon as I possibly can; Depends if I remember; Probably an hour; Maybe a week; After I get asked 10 times

God asks us to do things every day. We know what he is asking us to do when we read it in the Bible and when the Spirit of God speaks to us.

What is your response when you feel like God wants you to do something?

How long does it take you to jump into action when you feel like God wants you to do something?

There's more where that came from -God

When God asks you to do something, He does it for a reason. Can you think of a time you clearly thought God was asking you to do something?

Did you listen?

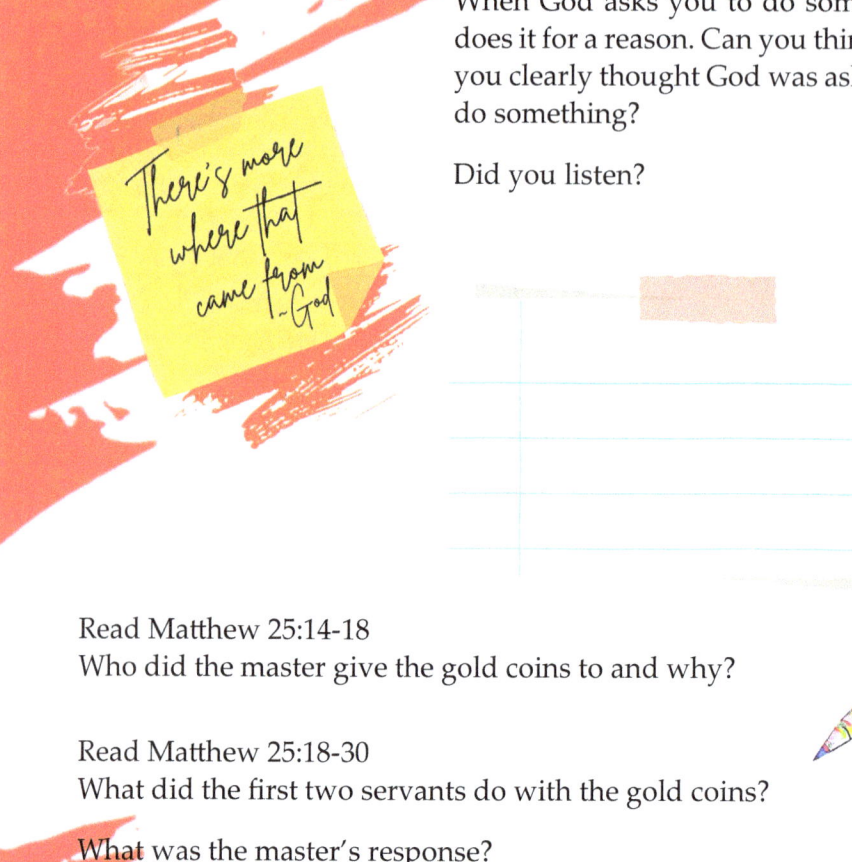

There's more where that came from ~God

Read Matthew 25:14-18
Who did the master give the gold coins to and why?

Read Matthew 25:18-30
What did the first two servants do with the gold coins?

What was the master's response?

What did the third servant do with the gold coins?

What was the master's response?

Read Matthew 25:23 again. Write in your own words what this verse means to you.

What prevents you from using what you have to honor God?

We already talked about how God gives us talents and abilities, passions and desires. He also gives us ideas!

What would happen if you act on the ideas that God places in your heart?

How could acting on God's ideas have a positive impact on you and the people around you?

Rip out this graphic and tape it to your mirror, your phone case, or inside your locker

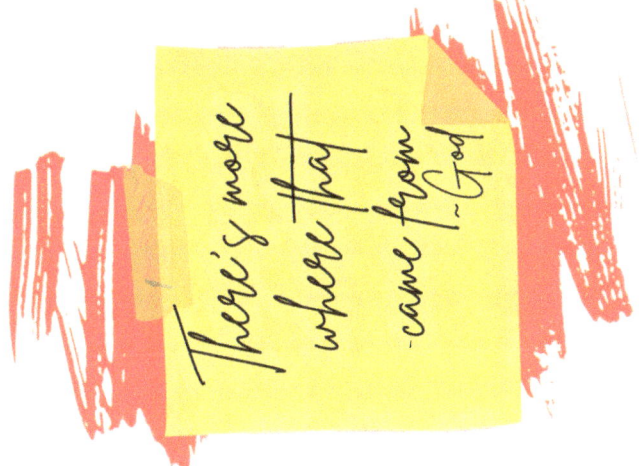

Chapter Five Notes

Chapter 6

Go M.A.D.

I've never been crazy about the expression "just a volunteer." The word "just" makes it sound like something is missing.

As a youth pastor, I've worked with a load of people, both within the church and in the community. I've never thought of anyone as *just* a volunteer. Our ministries are stronger, more effective, and probably a whole lot more fun because of the dedicated, talented, and sometimes crazy people who show up and make things happen.

The students in our youth programs were given plenty of opportunities to volunteer. They were learning about serving others and making a difference when I introduced them to Go Mad. "What's a Mad night?" the students would ask.

A Go Mad night was a new event I was starting with the teens. It was all about volunteering. I wanted to give our teens the opportunity to really live out some of the lessons that they had been learning on Friday nights. I wanted to give them a chance to go out in the world and "make a difference," or as we called it, Go M.A.D. On a Go Mad night, the students would be divided into smaller groups and head out into the community to lend a hand. One group set up a small library at a local school, while another volunteered to sort cans at the food bank. Sometimes, they babysat for single moms or shoveled snow for the elderly. At Christmas, they sang carols at Walmart while collecting food for hungry families. Planning activities that would allow the students to volunteer to help others with nothing in return had always been a part of leading youth ministry.

The high school youth group was called *Rooted*. One Go Mad night, the Rooted students created what is now known in our hometown as the community dinner. We called it the pop-up kitchen. It all started with a lesson and a challenge.

The lesson was found in the Bible in Matthew 25. It was a lesson about helping others. This lesson was followed by a challenge. The teens were divided into groups of 3 or 4 and asked to think about a need in the community. Then they were asked to create an event that we could do as a group to meet that need. I told them to be as creative as they wanted and not to let their ideas be limited by the size of our group or the size of our bank account. I've learned never to underestimate the power of a teenager's imagination. I asked them to be creative, and they did not disappoint.

This was more than a challenge for the teens. It was a competition. I told the groups we would take the winning idea and make it happen. I gathered up the papers with each group's ideas on them and took them home with me. Later that night, I went through the papers and saw an underlying theme. Almost every group had noticed families in our community that needed proper meals. Every group rose to the challenge of the Go Mad competition, but one group had really put their creative thinking caps on. This was their idea: *We should put on a free dinner for those in need, but not just a dinner: a sit-down dining experience. Not just a dining experience but a place to shop for free clothing while they wait to be served. Not just free clothing but free Bibles and Christian magazines as well.*

Ladies and gentlemen, we had a winner. I messaged the students to let them know the winning idea and that we would plan it at our next Go Mad night, and plan it we did! We found Nicky, a chef. Nicky had helped with fundraising dinners in the past. Some of the students got together with Nicky to plan a menu and figure out how much money we would need. Other students volunteered to take letters around town asking for donations. Others collected Bibles from a gentleman in our church who was connected with the Gideons. We chose a date, sent out posters, and made a Facebook post.

The night of the dinner, everything the students had imagined in their Go Mad challenge had become a reality. Everything was perfect, as long as you couldn't see behind the scenes. Behind the scenes, things were a little messy. OK, a whole lot messy. Our church was under construction, so we had booked the high school cafeteria for the dinner. Unfortunately, a snowstorm made it a school snow day, and they had to cancel our booking. Nicky arranged to cook the meal at her house. The teens drove to the church with loaded pots, pans, roasters, and slow cookers. I contacted the radio station, and they announced a last-minute change of location. We called in the church maintenance guy to help us with the ever-blowing fuses where the slow cookers and roasting pans were plugged in. The students quickly cleared away the chairs in the church and brought the tables out of storage. The center of the room had become a sit-down restaurant, complete with tablecloths and candy favors on each plate. Visitors could shop for free clothing donated from Walmart or soap and cleaning supplies donated from Shoppers Drug Mart. They could even pick up a new toothbrush courtesy of a local dentist.

Nicky and I had given a crash course on serving, and our visitors were treated to a dining experience complete with yes, sir and yes, ma'am. Our first dinner served only 30 people, but the students were not disappointed. They had nothing to compare it to and had no idea how many people to expect. The dinner was a hit. We decided that we would do it again whenever we had enough money. There was no specific time frame, just whenever we could; that led us to call it a pop-up kitchen. The more pop-up kitchens we did, the more guests started coming out.

While Nicky was stirring up things in the kitchen, God was stirring up things in the hearts of the people in our church.

Adults began asking to volunteer, and we appreciated the help. One couple in our church asked to cover the cost of the dinners so that we could make it a monthly event. When the construction on the kitchen was complete, the students would come after school on the last Friday of every month to set up tables, chop vegetables, make salads and juice, and set out donated clothes to give away. The Go Mad challenge would become a reality again.

It's been eight years since that group of 12 teen volunteers created the pop-up kitchen, now known as the community dinner. The dinner has become a staple in our community and part of the church's annual budget. They now have an amazing chef and a first-class group of kitchen volunteers that make 120 free meals at the end of each month.

Our teens served at every community dinner until Covid hit, and the dinners were switched to takeout. The idea was that the students would go make a difference, and they did!

The teens would hear me say over and over again, "You guys rock!" "Thank you so much." "You guys are amazing." "You're doing a great job," but I still wonder if these students have any idea just how valuable their volunteer work is. They are more than "just" a volunteer. They are individuals who serve God, serve others, and go M.A.D!

> *"The king replies by saying, 'Truly I tell you, whatever you did for one of the least of these brothers and sisters of mine, you did for me'" (Matthew 25:40 NIV).*

Read Chapter 6 of "The Spinning Mind of a Volunteer Youth Leader" for a more in-depth look at not being "just a volunteer."

Check off which of the following you would want to volunteer for?

Handing out food at a soup kitchen ☐ Keeping score at a kids' hockey game ☐ security guard at a rock concert ☐ babysitting for a single mom ☐ walking a neighbor's dog ☐ playing an instrument in a worship team ☐ supervising a bouncy castle ☐ flag person on a race car track ☐ shovel snow ☐ car wash ☐.

If you could volunteer anywhere, with anyone, for any activity or organization, what would it be?

Read Matthew 25:34-40.
What six things did the king say that the people had done for him?

Why were the people confused?

The king in these verses represents Jesus. Knowing that Jesus is the king in this parable and we are the people, what does verse 40 mean to you?

Read Colossians 3:23-24.
What does this verse in Colossians have in common with Matthew 25:34?

I'll never forget the day that I did this lesson in Bible college. It was my daughter's birthday. We didn't have close friends or family in the city with us, and Zip was away for work, so I did what any creative college mom would do. I threw a McDonald's birthday party—one three-year-old and ten university students celebrating a birthday over milkshakes and happy meals. As we left McDonald's that night, there was a homeless man sitting up against the wall beside the door. The man said, "Does anyone have spare change?" Well, he had said that to a group of Bible college students who had, that day, studied Matthew 25. We had just finished talking about serving those in need, feeding the hungry, taking care of the poor, and showing love to the people around us. We had just learned that what we do for others, we do for God. I was thinking, *man you have definitely come to the right place tonight*. All my study buddies jumped into action. Some ran inside and bought him hamburgers, some asked "What other needs do you have?" and some students started a deeper conversation about his life. I heard one of the students ask him what his name was, and he replied (I'm not making this up), "My name is Jesus." No way! Seriously, did our professor pay this guy to say that?

The response of a homeless man outside McDonald's, saying that his name was Jesus will always remind me that Jesus said, "What you do for the least of these brothers and sisters of mine you do for me."

Go mad – definition:
Make a difference serving God and the people in your community.

How could volunteering make a difference in your community?

How could volunteering make a difference in your church?

Plan your own Go M.A.D.
Make a list of 6 needs that you see in your own community.

GO M.A.D.

Create a plan that could help with one or more of these needs. Go ahead and brainstorm. Ifs are perfectly acceptable. Ex: If I had the money I would…. If I had the time….If I had help… Go ahead and add some ifs. Crazy is ok, too. Ex: This might sound crazy, but I would… Have fun with it. Ask yourself questions. If you need money, how could you raise it? If you need help, who might be onboard? If you need permission, where would you get it? Create your Go M.A.D. plan now!

MY GO M.A.D. PLAN

If you love the plan that you created and want to put it into action, go for it. Share your ideas with your friends, family, youth leaders, and anyone else who might be onboard. If the project seems overwhelming, don't worry about it. Do something small instead and see where God takes you next.

Prayer Break

Talk to God and ask him to give you a desire to serve Him and those around you. Pray that He will show you opportunities to help others and help you to go M.A.D. (make a difference) in your church and your community.

Chapter Six Notes

Chapter 7

The Spinning Mind

Originally, I titled this book, "Inside the Twisted Mind Of A Volunteer Youth Leader." I later changed it to *Spinning Mind* because twisted mind sounded a little too Joker from Batman, kind of creepy. Rest assured, I don't have a creepy Joker kind of twisted mind, but when I visualize what's going on in my head at any given time, it slightly resembles a mini tornado. Thoughts are flying around; I'm planning, organizing, scheduling, making lists on my mental notepad, replanning, reorganizing, rescheduling, and scratching things off that same mental notepad. It's a non-stop whirlwind of thoughts, a mental tornado. And that is where the twisted mind of a volunteer youth leader came from.

You would think I would want to turn it off, make a stop, clear my head, but no. I thrive in this kind of environment. It's not unorganized or chaotic; it's just an endless flow of thoughts moving through my mind, and for me, it's a three-step process. You think it, you plan it, you make it happen. I do things. I'm a doer. I don't know if that's a real word, but that's what I am, and it works for me. You know what *doesn't* work for me? Staying still. I've never been good at that.

Zip had some travel perks through his work, and

he took me on a vacation to Cuba. The resort was incredible, the food was amazing, perfect sandy beaches with an aqua-coloured ocean. The ultimate relaxation atmosphere, but not for me. I'd never been on vacation before, not like this. Anytime we had been away before, it always felt like taking care of the family but somewhere other than home. This was different. There were no kids to care for, no meals to make, and honestly, nothing to do but relax. Relaxing meant not thinking, not planning, and not making things happen. I am not wired that way.

The first morning at the resort, we headed to the beach, applied sunscreen, and made ourselves comfortable on some reclining lounge chairs. Tim pulled his hat down over his face and closed his eyes. After a minute of silence, I was ready to go. "Wanna walk on the beach?" I asked. "No, I just want to relax" was his reply. One minute later: "Wanna swim in the ocean?" "Nope, I just want to relax. Try it; just lay there and close your eyes." I tried; it was a no-go.

If doing nothing was relaxing, then relaxing was boring. I couldn't do it. Eventually, I headed back to the room to grab my camera. I joined Tim back on the lounge chairs and began taking snapshots. A snapshot of the ocean, a snapshot of a palm tree, a snapshot of Tim sleeping, a snapshot of my toes in the sand. I'd photograph anything as long as it meant that I didn't have to sit there and do nothing.

I know that taking time to relax and recharge is important. I just wasn't very good at it.

Several years ago, I took a group of students to Thunder Bay for a week-long mission trip. Planning a trip of any kind requires preparation, but one where the cars are loaded with teenagers, even more so. Having all the details lined up ahead of time was super important to me. I was connected with Jessica from the Centre in Thunder Bay. She was my contact person. We messaged back and forth several times to arrange for my group to spend the week volunteering at the Centre and helping in her community. As the trip got closer, there were more and more details to finalize, but Jessica got harder and harder to get ahold of. I tried to be understanding, knowing how much responsibility she had. She must've been extremely busy. I have to confess that as the days went on and the details of our trip were not finalized, I was growing impatient. I would call the office, but Jessica was never available. "I am sorry, but she's out of the office." "She's down by the river today." "She's gone on a hiking trip today." "You'll have to call her back; she's taking a quiet day on the mountain side." No joking; this was the response I got from her office.

I didn't get it. How could she take time off to sit by the river when she hadn't returned her emails yet? Why would she take time off to hike up a mountain when she hadn't finished making arrangements for the trip? The truth is, she wasn't taking time off. She was taking a time out. After getting to know Jessica during the mission trip, I had a better idea of what was really going on. Jessica's relationship with God was extremely important to her. She wanted every decision she made in ministry to be guided by the Holy Spirit, so she scheduled alone time with God. One-on-one quality God time by the river, on the hiking trail, or up the mountain.

You would think that, as a pastor, I would have been a little less judgmental when it came to someone wanting to spend some alone time with God. I mean, Jesus did the same thing, so it must not be a bad idea. Jesus took timeouts to have quality one-on-one time with God. This is exactly what Jessica from the Centre was doing. She wasn't avoiding my calls or neglecting my emails; she was busy—busy spending alone time with God.

I've preached it many times myself—the importance of being alone with God. One night, I had a conviction that I needed to practice what I preached. It wasn't unusual for me to wake up with a mind full of creative thoughts. I often prayed about things before I went to sleep, and God would answer my prayers in my dreams. If I was working on a message, I would wake up with pages of truly inspired words in my heart. If I was preparing a lesson or putting together a series, I would get a ton of ideas in the middle of the night;

super cool.

There were other times, however, when I had awakened in the middle of the night with a mini tornado of plans spinning in my head and thought, *not cool.* I just wanted to sleep, but I found myself putting notes in my phone of creative ideas that God was throwing at me.

The convicting realization that I needed to practice what I preached about spending time with God came around 3 am. It was another inspirational wake-up call of creative ideas, but this time, I prayed, "God, why? I love that you do this, but why at 3 AM????" I heard a very clear voice in my head say, "Because you won't stay still long enough during the day." Bam! That was powerful. It was a convicting realization that I needed to spend some alone time with God. I had no problem finding time to pray. I prayed in the car while I drove down the road. I prayed at the sink when I did the dishes; I even prayed in the shower. But I didn't set aside quiet time to listen for answers. If I wanted my youth ministry to be the best that it could be, and if I wanted a full night's sleep, I needed to set aside quiet time with God during the day—a relaxing, recharging timeout where I could hear God's voice over and above the mini-tornado spinning in the mind of this volunteer youth leader.

"Then, because so many people were coming and going

that they did not even have a chance to eat, he said to them, 'Come with me by yourselves to a quiet place and get some rest'" (Mark 6:31 NIV).

For more of Sarah Jane's Spinning Mind and the impact of spending alone time with God, read "The Spinning Mind of a Volunteer Youth Leader," chapter 7.

Do you have a spinning mind? Circle the answer that best applies to you.

-Yes, I have 50 tabs open that rotate continually in my brain.

-Yep, always, never a dull moment in my mind.

-Kinda, but my thoughts are pretty organized.

-Not really; I'm always thinking about something, but no tornado happening.

-No, it's pretty quiet up there!

Make a list of what spins in your mind. What do you spend time thinking about?

When was the last time you gave yourself a timeout?

When was your last quiet time with God?

In the New Testament, we see examples of Jesus taking timeouts with God.
Read Luke 5:15-16.

What was Jesus busy doing? (verse 15)

What did Jesus do next? (verse 16)

Read Luke 6:12-13.
What decision did Jesus have to make? (verse 13)

What did Jesus do before He made that decision? (verse12)

Read Matthew 14:22-27.
What amazing act was Jesus able to do? (verse 25)

What had Jesus done the night before? (verse 23)

In Luke 22, Jesus is arrested. He knows that He is going to be put to death for the sins of the world.
Read Luke 22:39-44.
What did Jesus do before He was arrested? (verse 39-41)

What happened when Jesus spent one-on-one prayer time with God? (verse 43)

We need to follow Jesus' example and set aside quiet time with God.

On a scale of 1-10, circle how easy or hard it would be for you to find quiet alone time to spend with God.

1 being super easy, "I'm never busy, and it's always quiet where I am." 10 being super hard, "I have no time to myself, and it's always crazy around me."

Read Mark 1:35-37.

What happened to Jesus when he tried to get some alone time?

Jesus was trying to get away. He was looking for some one-on-one quiet time with God, but Jesus was an important guy and people were always looking for Him. It couldn't have been easy for Jesus to find alone time to pray and listen to God, but He made it a priority.

Where can you find your own timeout space?

Find a quiet place to call your own, a place with no distractions. It could be a park bench, a hiking trail, a table in the library, or a quiet corner of the house; be creative. Where can you hide out and have an uninterrupted quiet time with God? No phone, no streaming media, no sister or brother knocking at the door. Find that place. Tell someone where it is so they don't think you've disappeared, and then use that space for your one-on-one time with God.

Prayer Break

Take a timeout, just you and God. Tell Him how you feel about whatever is happening in your life right now. Ask God to guide you and help you in your everyday activities and decisions. Take time to listen to God as He speaks to your heart.

Chapter Seven Notes

Chapter 8

I Like Your Focus

I was sitting in the eye doctor's chair, looking into a big, silver, binocular-shaped machine covered with spinning charts, levers, and gadgets. The doctor moved the gadgets back and forth. He got me to close one eye and then the other. It only took a few minutes before he said, "I see the problem; you're going to need glasses." A few weeks earlier, I had been on vacation, and in my spare time, I entertained myself with Sudoku puzzles. Whenever I worked on a puzzle, I would get a dull ache behind my eyes. The doctor said I wouldn't need glasses immediately, but within the year, I would need to pick up a pair. He said not to get anything expensive, just buy a cheap pair off the rack at a dollar store.

The year went by, and my eyes were fine. In fact, it was three years before I needed to take the doctor's advice. The dull ache was back. The next time I was at a dollar store, I checked out the glasses and even tried on a few pairs. I put on one pair, picked up a chocolate bar, and tried to read the fine print on the back of the wrapper. It worked; I could focus. I still didn't buy the glasses, but I did buy the chocolate bar. A couple of weeks later, I went back and picked up a pair of small frame, +1, leopar- print glasses because being able to focus is important. In youth ministry, that is exactly what I needed to do: focus. Games were fun, cool activities brought more kids out, field trips were exciting, and snacks always made things better, but the real focus needed to be on Jesus.

After leading a volunteer meeting to discuss our upcoming plans for children's ministry, one of the older teen guys saw me in the parking lot and said, "I really like your focus." I probably said something along the lines of "Cool, thank you, and thanks for your help." I was impressed with him. When I got home, I told Zip about the student who really paid attention in the meeting. I told Zip that he hadn't just paid attention to the activities and the schedule but to the purpose of our children's ministry. When I told Tim that this guy had liked my focus, Zip laughed and said, "He was probably just trying to tell you that he liked your car." I had to work that out in my head. It only took a second to realize that Zip was right. I had a new car. It was a gold-coloured Ford Focus.

I decided a few years ago to get my motorcycle license. Zip came home with a 2003 black Suzuki Marauder. It was a gift for our wedding anniversary. I started practicing in the yard. I practiced switching gears and turning back and forth between pylons in the driveway. I practiced coming to a stop and not stalling when I took off again. I could do all of these things, but there was one thing I could not do. I could not make a sharp turn. All I wanted to be able to do was go out the end of my driveway, turn around, and come back on the other side. But I couldn't make the turn. I couldn't seem to make it past the mailbox. I had three choices: hit the mailbox, hit the ditch, or stop the bike, push it back out, and try again. I chose option number three over and over again.

Finally, I decided that I was going to make this happen. I was going out on one side of the driveway and back on the other. I gave myself a pep talk and headed out of the yard. As I turned to come back into the driveway, I was looking right at the mailbox. It was getting closer and closer. All I had to do was go around it, just turn the bike a little bit sharper. And then it happened: mailbox versus motorcycle. The mailbox won. It was the first time I went down on my bike.

A few weeks later, I took a motorcycle training course. We did all the prep work, and then they put us on the bikes. The first thing the instructor did was set up the pylons in a tiny little circle. He instructed us to enter the circle, do a sharp turn, and come back out where we had entered. Seriously, the first thing is a sharp turn? I tried, but nope, wasn't going to happen. I came out on the wrong side of the circle every time.

The next day the instructor set up all the different parts of the course that we needed to complete in order to pass the exam. The more I practiced, the easier things got. I was able to do all the requirements except one. We needed to enter a sharp turn with pylons on either side, complete the turn, and exit the pylons at the other end. When we were on break, the instructor asked me how I was doing. I said I was struggling with the sharp turn. He said that he had noticed and that he had some advice for me. What he said next was profound. He pointed at the exit of the sharp turn. "If that is where you want to be, then you need to look over there." He went on to say, "Don't look at where you're going; turn your head and look at where you want to be." Wow, instructor dude, that's not a riding lesson; that's a life lesson. This is why I couldn't turn away from the mailbox, because it was the very thing I was focusing on. Lesson learned. Don't look at the mailbox in front of you; turn your head and look at where you want to be.

I got up to the line, put the bike in gear, turned my head, and looked at where I wanted to be. There stuck in the grass at the other end of the pylons was a Tim Hortons bag. I thought, *that's it; that's where I need to be.* I let go of the clutch, and I focused on that Tim Hortons bag. I did not take my eyes off it. I made the corner, and not just that one time. I would line up, turn my head, look at the Tim Hortons bag, and make the corner, line back up, turn my head, look at the Tim Hortons bag, and make the corner, over and over. After we finished practicing, we broke for lunch. When we returned to do the exam, someone had cleaned up the parking lot, or the wind blew really hard, because the Tim Hortons bag was gone. I told myself that I could handle this, that I knew what to do. I just had to remember not to look at the pylons in front of me but to turn my head and focus on where I wanted to be.

When we have a personal relationship with God, our focus should be on Jesus. Following Jesus is the direction that we need to take. But knowing that and doing it are two different things.

"But seek first his kingdom and his righteousness, and all these things will be given to you as well" (Matthew 6:33 NIV).

Read chapter 8 of "The Spinning Mind of a Volunteer Youth Leader" for more of Sarah Jane's "I Like Your Focus" experiences.

.

On a scale of 1-10, circle how much you focus on your relationship with Jesus. 1 being hardly ever, maybe in church sometimes. 10 being all the time, can't get it off my mind.

 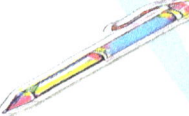

The motorcycle instructor's life lesson was not to focus on the pylons in front of you but on where you want to be. Don't look at what you're going through; look at what you're going to!
Check which of the following get in the way of your relationship with Jesus.

Distractions ☐ Temptations ☐ Fears ☐ Failures ☐ Other people's opinions ☐ Bad advice ☐ Other _____
Other _____

There are many pylons/distractions that keep us from focusing on Jesus. Right now, we will work our way through three of them.

Sometimes there is fear between where we are and where God is leading us. Check off which fears may stop you from following Jesus. ✓

Fear of rejection ☐ Fear of being alone ☐ Fear of the unknown ☐ Fear of failure ☐ Other_____ ☐

I am not an expert at dealing with fears. But God is.
Read 2 Timothy 1:7.
What has God not given us
What has He given us?

If you are experiencing fear, it's not coming from Jesus.
If you are standing face to face with fear, turn your face towards Jesus. Don't look at what you're going through; look at what you're going to!

It's easy to get caught up in our fears. It's a natural reaction. The world's reaction to fear is to focus on the negative and worry about what might or might not happen. But God says when you have a relationship with Him, then your reaction to fear can be different.

Read John 14:27. What does God give you that the world can't give you?

The world leads us into a state of panic, but God leads us into a state of peace.
Read the following verses and list what reasons they give for not being afraid.
Isaiah 41:10
Isaiah 41:13
Psalm 23:4
Psalm 27:1
Deuteronomy 31:6

Don't focus on your fear; focus on Jesus

There will be times in your life when you want to look to Jesus but focus on your failures instead.

We've all messed up, made mistakes, and failed at something. For example, we didn't make the team, didn't pass the test, didn't get the job, got dumped, or got fired. Failure is a part of life, but fear of failure doesn't have to be. We either get back up and try again, or we learn from it and move on.

What failures have you had in your past? How were you able to move on?

Read Psalm 37:23-24.

Romans 8:28

What do these verses say about failure?

Have you ever felt like you were failing in your relationship with God?

Have you ever found yourself thinking, *I tried to live a life that pleased God, but I messed it up. I tried to follow Jesus, but it was too hard. I tried to do the right thing, but it didn't happen. I tried not to sin, but I gave into temptation.*

Just for the record, none of this makes you a failure.

It doesn't matter what you've gone through or what mistakes you've made; you are not a failure.

You may fail at different things along the way, but God is a God of second chances.

Read 1 John 1:9 and Daniel 9:9

What do these verses say about forgiveness?

Your sins can be forgiven. That's why Jesus died on the cross.

Read Galatians 1:4.

God will continue to love you, forgive you, and help you every time you mess up. Don't focus on your failures; focus on Jesus.

DON'T *Focus on your Freak'in problems*
FOCUS ON JESUS

What problems do you struggle with?

If you can't think of any problems and you're crushing it right now, that's cool, but one day you will be faced with a problem, and you will have a choice to make. Will you focus on that problem, or will you focus on Jesus?

Read John 16:33.

What does this verse say about facing problems?

All the reasons God gave us not to be afraid in the "don't focus on your fears" section of the lesson are the same reasons He gives us not to focus on our problems. What are the reasons not to be afraid that also apply to not focusing on our problems?

Instead of telling God how big our problems are, tell your problems how big your God is.

Read Philippians 4:6, 1 Peter 5:7

How do these verses tell us to deal with our problems?

Don't focus on your problems; focus on Jesus.

Prayer Break

Think about what might stop you from following Jesus. Ask God to help you to stop focusing on those pylons/distractions and focus on Him. Ask God to help you overcome any fears you may have in your life. Take a moment to tell God that you believe in the power of forgiveness because Jesus died on the cross. Ask Him to forgive you for the sin you have in your life. Think of whatever problems you may be facing today and ask God to help you as you deal with those problems. Remember God is bigger than any problem you could ever face. Give God your fears, your failures, and your problems. Ask Him to help you focus on what you're going to instead of what you're going through.

Chapter Eight Notes

Chapter 9

Claiming My Title

I had a trusted friend once tell me that my level of confidence could probably be intimidating to some people. I thought, "My, what?" We were texting back and forth, and I typed L.O.L. But I did more than just type it. I was legitimately laughing out loud. I wasn't confident at all. I was competent, that was for sure. If I was given a job to do, I would do it, and I would do it well, but confident, not so much. No matter how good I was at my job, the question was always there. Am I good enough? I texted them back and said, "I'm laughing because that confidence is totally fake." I may have looked confident on the outside but was quiet and timid and a little insecure on the inside. That was the day I diagnosed myself with fake confidence syndrome. Apparently, fake confidence was something I had mastered.

I had never been an upfront, look-at-me, listen-to-me-speak, kind of person. Sitting at the back of the class and trying not to get noticed was more my thing. Actually, not the back of the class. Those were the seats saved for the stereotypical rebels. I was more of a sit-in-the-middle-of-the-room kind of person, right behind the class clown and the smarty-pants, but never at the front.

It's ironic how, as a pastor in youth ministry, it became my job to be at the front, speaking to teens, their parents, small groups, and large groups. I had literally become a public speaker.

The fact that I was quiet and shy didn't stop God from calling me into youth ministry. It didn't seem to matter that a typical youth pastor was a little louder and, at times, a whole lot crazier than me. I remember being at a northern youth event with nearly 100 students and a dozen youth leaders. The worship band was playing, and everyone was super hyped. I watched as youth leaders made their way to the front. They started jumping up and down and waving their arms in the air. Insecurity, a lack of confidence, or perhaps a little devil on my shoulder began to play with my mind, telling me, "That is what a real youth pastor should look like." But that wasn't me. It wasn't my personality. I didn't want to be upfront, and I didn't want to be jumping up and down. I'd given birth to four children, so if I had jumped up and down that dramatically, I probably would have peed my pants.

I knew that there were times in youth ministry when I was going to have to get out of my comfort zone, speak a little louder, and muster up some fake confidence, but this was not one of those times. It made no difference to my students if I was dancing at the front or giving them a high-five when they returned to their seats, yet it still made me question myself. I had a passion and a deep desire to work with students, but was I a real youth pastor?

My friend, a doctor, was telling me about something called impostor syndrome. Apparently, a lot of people in the medical field struggle with this. She said that impostor syndrome can make a person doubt themselves or suffer from a lack of confidence regardless of their years of education or experience. She said imposter syndrome can leave people asking themselves what they are doing there and telling themselves that they don't belong and that they are frauds. She had no idea how much I could relate to this. It didn't matter that I had my Biblical certificate or had been doing child or youth ministry since high school. There were still times when I asked myself, "Am I really good enough? Am I really spiritually strong enough?"

That is when I decided that it was time to claim my title. I was a real youth pastor, and I needed to knock that little devil off my shoulder and start answering those questions with the answers that had been the truth all along. I was good enough. I was strong enough. The Bible says that I can do all things when I do them through the strength that God has given me. This Bible verse, along with my experience in ministry, taught me that all I really needed to do was trust God. He called me into it, and He gave me everything I needed. When I needed to be strong, He made me strong. When I had to be creative, He flooded my mind with ideas. When it was time to make a tough decision, He gave me wisdom. When I needed to stop being quiet and timid, get up, and speak to a large group of people, God would give me the confidence to do it. Speaking to my local teens was never really a struggle for me; they were my comfort zone, but asking me to get up in front of a group of anyone else, well, that was a different story.

I liked writing messages, and I looked forward to sharing them. The truth is, I wanted to speak; I really did. I'd even get excited about it, regardless of how large the group would be. But that excitement only lasted until the night before. That's when I asked myself, "Why did I agree to this? What was I thinking?" I would be torn between wanting to do this and do it well and being so nervous that my hands were shaking, and butterflies were doing loops in my stomach. This is how I felt while I waited for my turn to go on stage. But that's when God would show up. He would give me everything I needed to do what he had called me to do. It would never fail that during the last worship song before I went up on stage, my hands would stop shaking, the butterflies in my stomach would fly away, and peace would come over me. I would say an unexplainable peace, but I could explain it. It was God's way of saying, "Move over, Sarah; Holy Spirit coming through."

Eventually, I began trusting that God would show up. I still had shaky hands and butterflies before a speaking engagement, but I knew that when the last worship song played that God would give me the confidence to do what he wanted me to do. I realized that the self-diagnosed fake confidence syndrome had never been fake confidence. In those moments, God gave me exactly what I needed to do the things that He was calling me to do.

"I can do all this through him who gives me strength" *(Philippians 4:13 NIV).*

Read chapter 10 in "The Spinning Mind of a Volunteer Youth Leader" to see how God continually showed up in a powerful way, helping Sarah Jane overcome her fake confidence syndrome and claim her title.

Check off which of the following best describes you: ✓

I'm mostly shy ☐ I'm pretty energetic ☐
I'm the class clown ☐ I'm outgoing ☐ I'm
super friendly ☐ I'm over friendly ☐ I'm
not so friendly ☐ I'm strong and silent ☐
I don't like being in front of people ☐ I love
being in front of people ☐ I'm a behind-
the-scenes kinda person ☐ I like to be the
star of the show ☐ I'm an attention seeker
☐ I'm bold and confident ☐ I sit in the
corner and hope no one notices me ☐.

We all have different personalities and different levels of confidence. No matter where your comfort zone is, I guarantee you that at some point God will call you out of that comfort zone, and if you let Him, He will use you in places that you may have never expected.

What kind of things make you nervous when it comes to doing what God asked you to do?

Read Ephesians 3:20
In chapter 4, Runway Ranch, we looked at this verse and the idea of God doing more than we could ever ask or imagine. This applies to what God can do through us as well. When God gives us something to do, he gives us the ability to do it, even if it goes beyond what we could ever ask or imagine for ourselves.

Moses is known as one of God's greatest messengers. He is the leader who brought God's people out of slavery in Egypt.

Read Exodus 3:11,4:1, 4:10, 4:13, 4:13. What was Moses' response when God first asked him to help his people escape from Egypt?

Gideon is known as a military leader, a judge, and a messenger from God who defeated enemy armies in battle.
Read Judges 6:15. What was Gideon's response when God first asked him to fight against his enemies?

Jeremiah was a messenger for God in a very difficult time. He lived a life of extreme hardship but left behind a message of hope for us today in the book of Jeremiah in the Bible.

Read Jeremiah 1:6. What was Jeremiah's response when God chose him as a messenger to speak to God's people?

In the Old Testament, the Spirit of God would come upon certain people at certain times to give them the ability to do whatever it was that God asked them to do, even if it was out of their comfort zone or beyond their known abilities.

Read Exodus 3:12, 4:12, 4:14-17
What did the Spirit of God do to help Moses?

Read Judges 6:12, 6:16
What did the Spirit of God do to help Gideon?

Read Jeremiah 1:7-9.
What did The Spirit of God do to help Jeremiah?

When God asks you to do something specific, you may feel the same way Moses, Gideon or Jeremiah did: not good enough, not strong enough, not wise enough, not old enough (Warning: big *but* coming through), BUT when God asks you to do something, He gives you whatever ability you need to do it.

After Jesus' death on the cross, the Spirit of God became available to all believers.

Read John 14:26. What does Jesus say that the Holy Spirit will do for us?

Read and rewrite Philippians 2:13 in your own words.

Remember, when God gives us something to do, he gives us the ability to do it, even if it goes beyond what we could ever ask or imagine.

Prayer Break

Talk to God. Ask Him to help you to follow Him and accept the challenges He gives you even if they lead you out of your comfort zone. Ask God to show you if there is anything specific that He would like you to do today.

Chapter Nine Notes

Chapter 10

Righteous Right Hand

If you look really hard in the storage room in my basement, you'll find an old 80s-style school bag. In the bag, you will find 120 yo-yos of various sizes, shapes, and colours. My yo-yo collection used to be in a display case, proudly displayed on the walls of our apartments. As we moved from one town to another, the yo-yos eventually ended up in a bag, and the glass in the display case was broken. I started collecting yo-yos when I worked at camp as a teenager. Everyone had a thing. For one person, it was their crazy sunglasses, for another, their bright yellow Sun Zinc lips, and someone else sported fancy shoelaces. For me, it was my yo-yo. I found my first yo-yo on the ground after the campers left one Saturday. My second yo-yo came from the lost and found. For a while, I was a master of the yo-yo. I could rock the cradle, walk the dog, go around the world and back again. My only yo-yo trick today would be trying not to hit myself in the head when the yo-yo bounces back up the string.

I was known for saying two things that summer. Actually, singing one of them and saying the other. To the tune of *Row, Row, Row Your Boat*, I would sing, "Yo, yo, yo your yo-yo up and down the string, merrily, merrily, merrily, merrily, life is a wonderful thing." I was working with children at the time, so I guess it's OK that this sounds extremely childish to me now. My other saying was, "Life is like a yo-yo; sometimes you're up, sometimes you're down." At the beginning of my youth ministry, this is exactly how I felt. One Friday night, I would walk away on top of the world, a spiritual high. The students would have invited friends, and it seemed like everyone understood the message. Another time, I would walk away shaking my head and asking myself, "Why do I even bother?"

Working with youth can be exciting; it's fun. Teenagers are the most creative and witty people on our planet. The teens I work with say and do the weirdest things. They dance like no one's watching in a room full of people. They make me laugh even when I'm trying to be serious. They are smart. They are brave. They are stronger than they even know. But these same teenagers wake up every day to face some really dark realities. Life isn't always easy; sometimes it's hard, really hard, and teenagers experience that firsthand. I've worked with teenagers from broken homes, teens caught up in addiction, victims of abuse or neglect, and others who suffer from depression or anxiety. Their loads are heavy. There were very few times that I didn't feel the weight of their struggles.

When I pray for people, I have a habit of starting out my prayer by lifting them up to God. For example, if

I was praying for someone named Sue, I would pray, "Dear God, I want to lift Sue up to you right now." If I was praying for someone named George, I might say, "God, I'm lifting George up to you." I guess it was my way of saying that I was giving them to Him for help. One night I was praying for our youth group, not individuals, but the entire youth ministry as a whole. I just started out by saying, "Dear God, I am lifting up this youth group to you," and then I had a vision, one that completely changed the way I view youth ministry.

In the vision, there was a giant hand, a strong hand with a firm grip. It was holding up a serving tray or a plate of some kind. On top of the tray was a group of teens. The tray hung over the side of the hand, and hanging off the tray was another person. They weren't actually hanging off the tray. They were underneath the edge of it with their hands lifted up as if they were holding up the tray full of students, but they weren't. Their feet were dangling in the air. A second hand came down, and, using the pointer finger and thumb, it picked up the person dangling under the tray and placed them on top with a group of teens. I knew exactly what it meant. That was me. I was the person dangling underneath the tray, trying to hold it up. I heard a quiet whisper. "You don't hold up this youth group; I do." In the vision, God had picked me up and put me on the tray. He was carrying the weight. I couldn't lift this youth group up to Him because he was already holding us in His hand.

Whenever I think about this, I remember what the Bible says in Isaiah 41:10 that God "will strengthen you and help you. I will uphold you with my righteous right hand." I had seen the righteous right hand of God in my vision. The image was powerful. I didn't need to carry the weight of youth ministry on my shoulders when God was carrying it in His hand. I've heard people say that God won't give you more than you can handle, or in the middle of an overwhelming challenge, they'll say, "You got this," but sometimes I didn't "have this." I couldn't handle things on my own, and I didn't have to. I was never really on my own. God was holding me up with His righteousness right hand.

I have been asked many times, "How do you manage to do all this?" I don't know if I was asked because of the children's programs and youth activities I had been running or because I had four children wrapped around my legs. Being asked that question reminded me of an old hymn we used to sing in church. It was written over 100 years ago. If you dusted off an old songbook, you'd probably find it in there. I didn't pay much attention to the lyrics when I sang them in church as a kid, but I think about them now. The song was "He Giveth More Grace." It was about how when we're tapped out and have no strength left, God's strength is only beginning.

When we have exhausted our store of endurance,
When our strength has failed ere the day is half done,
When we reach the end of our hoarded resources
Our Father's full giving is only begun.

I decided that if anyone else asked me, "How do I do it?" I'd just say, "When we reach the end of our hoarded resources, our Father's full giving is only begun." They might have no clue what I was talking about, but it would be fun to say.

There was some real truth in those lyrics. If I wasn't strong enough, it didn't matter because God was. It was His righteous right hand that was holding me up.

"So do not fear, for I am with you; do not be dismayed, for I am your God. I will strengthen you and help you; I will uphold you with my righteous right hand" (Isaiah 41:10).

Read chapter 11 of "The Spinning Mind of a Volunteer Youth Leader" for more examples of the powerful and righteous right hand of God.

Circle below how strong you feel when life gets hard?

◉I feel weak and falling apart

◉I feel like I could use some help

◉I feel like I can tough it out on my own

◉I feel like I have the strength of a bodybuilder

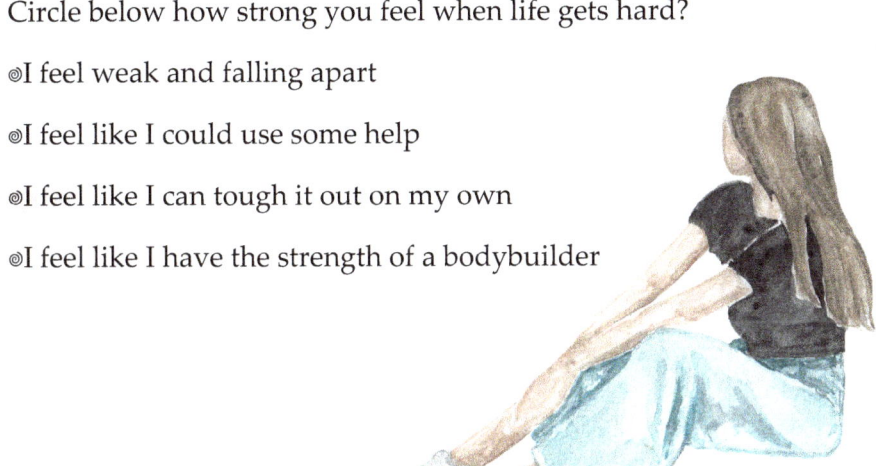

Read John 16:33
What does this verse say about having troubles in this world?

Make a list of the hardships that you and people you know face every day.

In our last chapter, we talked about how God will give you the strength you need to do the things that He has asked you to do. But that's not all. God can also give you the strength to make it through each day, even the really tough days when you feel like you can't go on.

Read Isaiah 40:29-31

What does God give to the weary?

Whose power does God increase?

What does Isaiah 40:31 say about renewing our strength?

Read Matthew 11:28
What will God give you when you come to Him with your problems?

Read 1 Peter 5:7
What should you do when you are feeling overwhelmed?

So do not fear, for I am with you;
do not be dismayed, for I am your God.
I will strengthen you and help you;
I will uphold you with my righteous right hand.
Isaiah 41:10

Righteous Right Hand

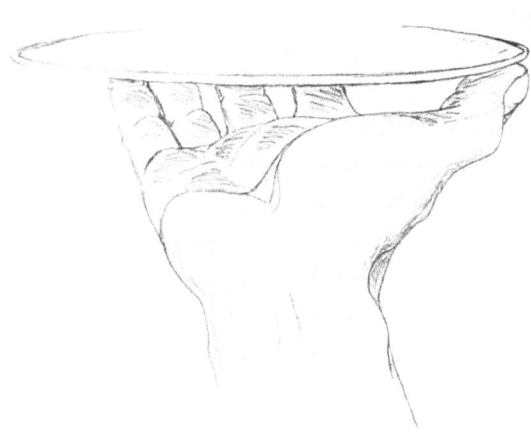

In what area of your life do you need God to hold you up?
Write or draw on top of the hand the things that you need God to help you with.

Prayer Break

Talk to God. Thank God for always being with you. Be real with Him and tell Him everything that you struggle with in life. Ask God to give you the strength you need to face every day even when things get tough. Take time every day to ask God to renew your strength.

Chapter Ten Notes

Chapter 11

They Can Hear You

"Your son doesn't pay attention in class," the teacher said. Not exactly how you want a parent-teacher interview to start off. "But he hears everything I say." Oh, ok, that sounded better. The teacher explained how my son Braxton always seems distracted in class. She often saw him staring out the window, drawing in his books, or playing with his shoelaces. She assumed he wasn't listening. He didn't keep eye contact with her and definitely was not hanging off every word she said. It was as if he was in his own world. She said, "I don't know how he does it; if I ask him what we're talking about, he always knows." She thought that he wasn't listening, but he was. He heard and remembered everything she said.

I am normally a pretty quiet person with not a whole lot to say, but when it comes to youth ministry and speaking with the teens, you couldn't get me to stop talking. I could spend hours preparing a powerful message, a lesson that packs a punch, or an inspirational speech. Yet I would often find myself asking, are they really? Are the messages really powerful? Do the lessons really pack a punch? Was that speech really inspirational? Do the words that I speak make an impact? Does my ministry make a difference in the lives of the students that I work with? At the end of the day, do they hear me and remember anything I say? Maybe you've asked yourself the same question: are my words powerful? The answer is yes! Someone is listening to you, and your words do have the power to make a difference.

I didn't think that James was listening. James was a part of Rooted Youth Ministry for several years. He often wandered off for months at a time but always managed to find his way back. After camp each summer, the students were given the opportunity on a Sunday morning to take the mic. They were asked to share stories from their week away. When it was James' turn to share a story, he didn't talk about camp. He talked about Rooted Youth and how it had been like a family to him. He said that Sarah (that's me) had said something earlier in the summer that had a huge impact on his life. James was quite the character, and I had no idea what would come out of his mouth, but I was even more curious about what had come out of mine. What did I say to him? My mind raced back over the last month to try and remember any deep, meaningful conversation I may have had with James. I couldn't remember any profound wisdom or sound advice I had given him. Now I was really curious.

He spoke directly into the mic and said, "Sarah told me that she was proud of me," then he said, "No one has ever told me that before." Wow, I couldn't even remember telling James that I was proud of him, but it definitely was something I would have thought, and I'm glad I shared my thoughts with him. Clearly, he was listening. The Bible says that the tongue has the power of life or death. Our words can speak life or death into the people around us. Telling James that I was proud of him was not a big deal to me; I didn't even remember saying it. But those words spoke life into James's situation.

I was on the phone with a young woman the other day. She was a part of our youth program growing up and still gives me a call when she's going through hard times. This young lady shared with me her heartache and her trouble. Then she told me that when she's really going through a difficult time, she thinks of this poem. She had memorized the poem and recited it over the phone for me.

> *From a child to a woman*
> *All fast forward no rewind*
> *See your moment in the future*
> *Leave the hurt and scars behind*
> *Standing in the mirror*
> *See the pain of yesterday*
> *Letting go and stepping forward*
> *Let forgiveness lead the way*

I said, "I like it; that's a pretty good poem." She started to laugh just a little. I said, "What? It's got a powerful message. Why are you laughing? Did you write it?" She said, "No, you did." She was right. I had written that poem for her many years before. I had forgotten about it, but she had not and had memorized every word. It wasn't a spoken word; it was a written word, but the results were the same. If she had never told me about it, I would not have known that those words were an inspiration for her so many years later. Sometimes we need to be reminded that someone is listening and that our words make a difference.

I have a secret drawer under my bed. The drawer itself is not a secret. It's my T-shirt drawer, no mystery there, but I've never told anyone what's tucked away behind the T-shirts. Hidden away behind the T-shirts is a stack of letters, a collection of thank you notes from some of the teenagers that were in the youth program. It's been a really long time since one of the teens passed me a handwritten thank-you note. My thank-yous now come in the form of a text, an Instagram message, or a funny "couldn't do it without you" GIF or meme. I don't make it a habit of saving texts or memes, but I did save those letters. If I ever ask myself if what I'm doing makes a difference, if anyone is listening, I just have to read some of the words on the pages of those letters. In many of these thank you letters, texts, or conversations, there seemed to be a recurring theme that I had somehow changed their lives. But the truth is, I didn't do that. I may have taught them things they needed to know. I may have encouraged them or challenged them. For some, I may have held them while they cried, but I didn't change their lives. God did that! Nothing I have ever said or will ever say will be as powerful as the word of God. God's word, His promises, His lessons, His truths, His messages, that's where the powerful words really are. When I say God's words, I'm talking about solid biblical truth. That's what changes lives! It's encouraging to know that telling James that I was proud of him impacted his life or that a poem I wrote for a student many years ago still brings her comfort today. Those thank-you letters tucked away in the back of my T-shirt drawer remind me that someone is listening. When I talk about God's love, teach about Jesus, speak on forgiveness, and preach the word of God, things change because God begins to work in the lives of the students who are listening. And yes, they are listening, and my words do make a difference.

"Do not let any unwholesome talk come out of your mouths, but only what is helpful for building others up according to their needs, that it may benefit those who listen" (Ephesians 4:29).

For more on the ability of your words to make a difference and the power of God's word to change lives, read chapter 11 in "The Spinning Mind of a Volunteer Youth Leader."

Fill these word bubbles with both positive and negative words or sayings that you might hear throughout your day.

Take a tube of toothpaste and squeeze half of it onto a plate (no, don't steal your family toothpaste tube without asking). Now, try your best to put the toothpaste back into the tube. It's not easy! It's very hard to do without leaving a mess behind. Same thing with your words. Be careful what you say. Hurtful words are hard to take back and usually leave a mess behind.

Your words have power. They have the power to help or hurt others, to build people up or tear them down, to break someone's heart or heal a broken one. Never underestimate the power of your words.

Read Proverbs 18:21. How powerful does this verse say that your words can be?

Read Colossians 3:8. Make a list of the things we should not be using our words for.

Read Proverbs 12:18. What difference can being reckless or wise with your words make?

Read James 3:9-10. What two kinds of words should not come out of the same mouth?

Read Proverbs 16:24. What kind of words have healing power?

Your words are extremely powerful.

What does Ephesians 4:29 say that we should be using our words for?

You may have a hard time believing it, but your words have a huge influence on the people around you.

Make a list of the people or groups that hear your words throughout the week.

Your words have the power to make a difference in their lives.

Cut out the note/envelope provided to send an encouraging note to someone. Fill the entire page or simply use a few powerful words. Choose a friend, a teacher, a family member, a janitor, a cashier, the guy at the taco place, whoever you want, you pick. Think of someone that you would like to encourage with your words and give them this note.

Maybe you've asked yourself this question: are my words powerful? The answer is yes! Someone is listening to you, and your words do have the power to make a difference.

Prayer Break

Talk to God. Ask God to help you watch your words. Ask Him to remind you to use encouraging words for others and to show how to use the power of your words to make a difference for others.

Chapter Eleven Notes

Chapter 12

Expectations vs Reality

We were sitting at a round table in the Life Centre, an addition to the church built several years earlier. This is where the new pastor and I held our staff meetings every Tuesday morning. We would discuss the week gone by, and I would fill him in on the schedule for upcoming youth events. That Tuesday morning, I told the pastor about a plan that had been in the works for a long time.

It had been almost 16 years since I started the youth program in Kapuskasing. I had loved students, cared about them, and prayed for them for years. I had prepared countless messages, lessons, and Bible series. I had planned youth events, Friday night activities, evening drop-ins, weekend adventures, mission trips, and so much more. Almost 16 years of doing what I truly loved to do. But it was time to let it go.

The pastor seemed surprised to hear that I would be leaving the ministry. It was never meant to be a surprise. It was no secret that my youngest son Levi's final year of high school would be my final year working with the students. My passion for youth ministry hadn't faded, and neither had my love for the teens. My deep desire to see their lives impacted through youth ministry had not changed. It was my plans that had changed.

Zip was now working for Sunwing in Toronto. He was in the sky more than on the ground, traveling from one vacation destination to another. If someone else was running the youth program, I could travel with him and visit a few vacation destinations myself. Victoria, now an adult, lived nine hours away. If I handed the youth ministry over to someone else, I could use Zip's discount flights to finally spend more time with her.

I like planning ahead. That's the kind of person I am. I plan things in advance and make to-do lists. That's how I get things done. I put them on a list, and then I make them happen. I like to-do lists so much that if I've done something that's not on my list, I will add it just so I can cross it off. Yes, I realize I probably need therapy for my to-do list addiction, but it works for me. Stepping out of youth ministry when Levi, our youngest, stepped out of high school was on my mental to-do list.

I let the pastor know that in a year and a half, I would be transitioning out of my position as youth pastor. I had a plan. Braxton, our middle son, would be away at university. Levi would be off to college. Benjamin might miss the home-cooked meals and piles of washed and folded laundry on his bed when he came home from work, but he was pretty much an adult and didn't need me to take care of him. When my time in youth ministry was over, I was going to travel—hit the skies with my favorite pilot and stop in for some quality time with my daughter.

What happened next was a clear case of expectations vs. reality. My expectation was that this plan was really going to happen. The reality was very different. Braxton came home after his first year at university and Levi decided to do a victory lap to get in one more year of high school basketball before he went to college. The Covid pandemic took my husband from full-time pilot to full-time farmer in a matter of months. He had lost his job at Sunwing. No more vacation destinations and no more cheap flights to see Victoria. This was the reality. The house wasn't empty, it was full, and the only traveling that Zip was doing was back and forth across the field in a tractor.

Several months passed, and people started asking questions. One of the hardest questions to answer was, "Why are you giving up youth ministry?" If someone had asked me that a year before, I could've told them all about the wonderful plans I had for the next stage of my life. But now, not only was that question hard, but it broke my heart a little more every time someone asked. I didn't have an answer. I started asking myself the same question, "Why *am* I giving up youth ministry?" I loved my students and loved spending time with them, planning, organizing, and teaching about

Jesus. If I wasn't going to be traveling and I was going to be home, then why was I giving it up? That was a *really* good question. The Bible teaches that God has plans for us and that those plans are good. I had to believe God had a plan because I certainly did not. I was taken back to the 'jump off the page' moment in the high school library and Miss White's English assignment asking what we wanted to do with our lives. I had discovered what the grown-up version of a camp counselor was. It was a youth pastor, and that's what I was. I became painfully aware that in just a few months, I would be giving up my dream job.

We were going through the process of selecting a new youth leader and considered that God might raise up someone from within the church. One person's name kept coming to my mind. His name was Shawn, and he was already helping with our junior high pro-gram. I could see that he was serious about ministry and his relationship with God. I thought Shawn might do a good job in youth ministry, but I tried not to think about it too much. I was really struggling with the idea of leaving youth work. Was this God's plan for me, or was I on my own in this? Was I following where God was leading me, or was I only leaving youth ministry because it was on my mental to-do list from years ago? And if I was following God, then why was it so hard? I had a whirlwind of thoughts spinning in my head. I felt guilty for abandoning the youth, selfish for making my own plans, and thankful for the opportunity to work with so many amazing teenagers, but heartbroken over saying goodbye. One Sunday morning I stood with my hands out to God; I couldn't hold back the tears. I was crying. My heart was aching. I'm just going to call it like it was. I was full-out throwing myself a pity party, but the emotions were real. I hadn't even stepped away from youth ministry yet, but I was missing it already. I stood there, wiping away the tears as I prayed.

That's when I heard God speak. The unmistakable voice of God said, "It's not about you." I turned my head slightly to the right, and Shawn was in the row in front of me. His arms were raised in the air as he worshiped God. It wasn't about me. It was about him.

That was a defining moment. That was the moment I stopped feeling sorry for myself. I stopped questioning if I had made the right choice. It was at that moment that I stopped feeling guilty and selfish at the same time. It wasn't about me. It never had been about me. It wasn't my youth ministry. It was God's, and it was time for someone else to lead it. Shawn had not been hired as our next youth leader, but I knew he would be.

It had been 29 years since I felt God calling me to work with teenagers as I sat at the table in the high school library. He led me on an amazing journey through youth ministry. I felt His presence, heard His voice, and saw Him come alive in the lives of the teenagers I worked with. I had learned to trust Him as He gave me the strength to do what He had called me to do. I didn't know what was next. For the first time in a very long time, I didn't have a plan. I needed to trust that God did. Sometimes my students would struggle with life plans, panicking if they had almost finished high school and hadn't decided on their future. I told them, "When you have no idea what you want to do next in your life, then you are in the perfect place for God to call you into something that you may never have thought of on your own." I was in that place. The perfect place for God to put another "jump off the page" word in my life.

"Commit to the LORD whatever you do, and he will establish your plans" (Proverbs 16:3).

Read Chapter 13, 'It's Not About You', in "The Spinning Mind of a Volunteer Youth Leader," for more on Sarah Jane's expectations vs. reality moment and learning to follow God's plan even when you don't know what's next.

Have you ever had an expectations vs. reality moment in your life where you had a plan but things didn't work out?

NO   YES   What happened?

Someday you will.

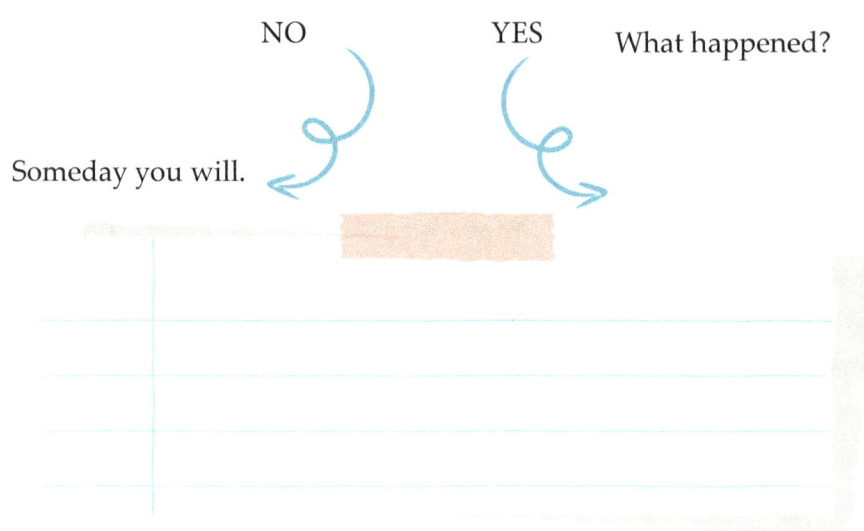

When our plans don't work out the way that we expected, we can still trust that even if we don't have a plan, God does!

Have a brother, sister, parent, or friend blindfold you. Using only their words, ask this person to lead you through your home or backyard, being careful not to allow you to trip on objects, fall down the stairs, or smack into any walls.

How did it feel to be moving but not see where you were going?

Did you trust the person leading you?

Flashback

In parts one and two of this study, we learned that God has a plan for you. Read John 3:16, 1 John 1:9.
Where does God's plan for you start?

Match the following verses with God's everyday plan for your life.

Matthew 22:37	Do good, be a light for others.
Matthew 5:16	Praise God.
1 Peter 5:6-7	Humble yourself, give Him your concerns.
1 Peter 2:9	Pray and be thankful.
1 Corinthians 10:31	Love God.
1 Thessalonians 5:16-18	Honour God in EVERYTHING.

Knowing God's everyday plan for your life is easy; it's written in the verses listed above. Knowing God's specific plan for you in the future is a different story. Sometimes following Jesus is like moving forward with a blindfold on. We need to trust him even if we can't see where we are going.

What does 2 Corinthians 5:7 say about not knowing what's next?

"When you have no idea what you want to do next in your life, then you are in the perfect place for God to call you into something that you may never have thought of on your own."

~Sarah Jane

Using your own words, what do you think that this quote means?

What does Proverbs 16:3 say about making plans for the future?

When you are following God and trusting Him, He will lead you and help you to make plans that line up with His will for your life.

Flashback

In part 2 we looked at Proverbs 3:5-6. What three things does this verse tell you that you should do if you want God to direct your path?

Read Jeremiah 29:11.
What kind of plan does God have for you?
As you start out or continue on your journey, following God's plan for your life, it is my prayer that you will feel His presence, hear His voice, and learn to trust Him. I pray that you will be filled with His strength as you do whatever it is that He has called you to do. Even if you never have a 'jumpin' off the page' experience in your life, I pray that you will always remember that God *does* have a plan for you, and it is good!

Prayer Break

Spend some one-on-one time with God. Ask Him to give you the faith you need to follow Him even when you can't see what next.

Chapter Twelve Notes